How To Teach Daily Living Skills to Adults with Developmental Disabilities

John Meyers

iUniverse, Inc.
New York   Bloomington

How To Teach Daily Living Skills to Adults with Developmental Disabilities

iUniverse books may be ordered through booksellers or by contacting:

iUniverse
1663 Liberty Drive
Bloomington, IN 47403
www.iuniverse.com
1-800-Authors (1-800-288-4677)

ISBN: 9-781-4401-1319-2 (pbk)
ISBN: 9-781-4401-1320-8 (ebk)

Printed in the United States of America

iUniverse rev. date: 12/29/2008

Chapter 1 – Labels

Right from the get-go let me state that I am not an expert in the field of developmental disabilities. I don't have a doctorate in anything. I don't even play a doctorate on TV. I'm just a guy who has worked in the field of developmental disabilities for about 16 years. My current position is Site Director. Oh, my gosh!… a label… well, more about that in a minute. One of my previous labels was "fireman" for 12 years or so. I have the label as an "entertainer", too, because my wife and I have done quite a bit of writing and acting and singing in the past. I've been labeled lots of things by lots of people and yet, somehow, I manage to struggle on.

The site I am directing (to fulfill my current label) is a day program providing social and behavioral skills training for adults with developmental disabilities. Since I work with adults, my approach in this book will be from the perspective of working with adults with developmental disabilities. Oh, and a disclaimer: I will be painting with a broad brush to give you some basic principles – every principle I talk about may not apply to every individual with a developmental disability.

I am both amused and frustrated with the rush by many to jump on the current bandwagon of denigrating day programs and to push adults with disabilities into "less restrictive" activities. The current thinking seems to be that day programs pretty much do nothing to prepare an individual with a developmental disability for independent living. Really?

Let's look at the story of Bob, a 35 year old man working in an enclave. He lives with the label of "employee" and spends his days sitting alone in a cubicle at a desk making phone calls to people he doesn't even know. There are a whole bunch of people in these cubicles around him. He is paid minimum wage (thus adding to his labeling as a person of minimal worth), and is expected to fulfill quotas of work performance placed upon him by others. His "wage" was determined on the basis of a two page self-written application and a 30 minute interview by a single interviewer who had never even met Bob before. If Bob asks for a raise, he is reminded that his job is an "entry level position" which seems to place less value on his abilities.

Once per year Bob is subjected to an evaluation by a staff person who doesn't know Bob well, but bases his evaluation on data collection of Bob's productivity levels. From this evaluation, goals are set for his performance for the coming year. Bob is not allowed to invite his support team (friends, family, etc.) to attend the goal setting meetings prior to his evaluation. Bob himself isn't even allowed to attend the goal setting sessions. He hears about the vocational goals set for him at his single evaluation meeting which is held at the time and location that is most convenient to his head staff person.

Bob hasn't been allowed a raise in three years because he has been labeled (by his head staff person during Bob's evaluation session) as being a "problem employee" and having a dysfunctional behavior which causes him to spend more time surfing the internet than the others in Bob's vocational group thus limiting the amount of time he spends making phone calls.

Bob is crowded in with other people who have the same "employee" label as himself, and who dress as he does every day. He is required to wear a tie even though it chafes at his neck and is an irritant. He is not allowed to listen to his favorite music while at his desk or to keep personal items such as an open bag of chips and a coke on his desk.

He is required to spend his days in the same windowless space for 8 hours with only a 15 minute break twice a day and a one hour limit lunch time. His workplace is in a business park away from downtown areas where other people congregate during the day, but his job is still considered "community based."

Bob is not allowed visitors during the day and his work space is open to inspection by staff people over him without invitation. He is told what time to arrive at work, what time to take his breaks, when to break for lunch (where he is expected to go eat with others in a large room full of people who are expected to eat their lunch at the same time), and when to go home.

Damned sheltered workshops. How can you teach anyone about "real world" employment this way? This is simply outrageous!

Actually that story sounds like most of my non-disabled friends working in the "real world." Wait a minute... that's my cousin Bob I just described.

Oh, and there I used a label again... my "non-disabled friends." Of course I don't refer to them as my "non-disabled friends." I just call them, my friends. That's how I label them to keep the straight from my "enemies." Come to think about it, I don't call the clients in my program "disabled clients," either. They're just clients. We call them clients to keep them straight from our "staff." Although the current national label is "consumer" because someone decided that "client" was a label and we shouldn't use labels. The consumers in our program recently voted at their Client Association meeting to call themselves "clients" (which is why it's called the "Client Association"), so that's what I'll go with.

I recently read a book where someone was decrying the

use of labels like "mild," "moderate," "severe," and "profound" as labels for mental retardation. The author was very upset over the use of labels like that which only serve to perpetuate the social stigma attached to such words. His solution was to come up with new words for the same categories. Some people just have too much time on their hands. It reminds me of the entertainer who wanted to be known as "The Entertainer Formerly Known As"… then changed his name to a symbol… but no one could pronounce a symbol, so he changed back to whatever it was. All that certainly got him a lot of attention in the media, but it didn't change who he was and how good of an entertainer he was.

You can call me a Site Director, or a fireman, or an entertainer… just don't call me late for supper. I have better things to do than sit around and worry about labels. I have a day program to run.

I suppose the day program I run is pretty typical. I haven't visited a lot of other day programs across the country; I've visited a few and I've read about lots of them and talked to some people who work in some of them. Some programs sound pretty good. Some of them sound pretty boring. The program I work for used to be boring. I almost quit right after I started because it was so boring. I started out as a line staff (darned labels!) making minimum wage. Years later some things haven't changed. Now we start our line staff a few cents above minimum wage. We're a private non-profit agency that is state funded. One thing that *has* changed is what we do with our time during the day.

When I started, our day program for adults with developmental disabilities had over 100 clients in one building. We spent our days on crisis control and babysitting. We were called "Behavior Trainers" then. But when you have over 100 clients and close to 50 staff people in the same building, I'm not sure whose behavior was being trained… theirs or ours. I just know it killed me to sit in a room with a group for six hours and wonder if the batteries in the clock were dying and that's why the hands moved so slowly.

Our staff are on their third label since I started with my current agency: Behavior Trainer to Inclusion Specialist to the current label, Life Skills Coach. They still do the same job no matter what we call them. I'm sure that eventually we'll find a label that makes them better employees... oh, wait... employees... that's a label, too. Darn!

Fortunately, someone noticed my obvious talents and I quickly started moving up the ranks. The huge amount of staff turnover may have something to do with that, but don't burst my bubble. I became a "Lead Trainer," then a "Division Manager," "Division Coordinator," and then the "Client Services Coordinator," and "Resource Specialist," and finally capping my career with the title (I mean label) of "Site Director." My mother would have been so proud.

When I became a Site Director, the first thing I did was re-write our new employee orientation book. My Executive Director (wow, the world is just full of labels) may not like to hear this, but we used to throw staff to the wolves. We had a full week of watching outdated videos, listening to some people read to us, and reading lots of stuff with big words by ourselves, then we were put in a room with our clients. No one even wished us "good luck." The first thing I did was walk out of my orientation and meet up with a woman who asked me to please write down a note for her. I was happy to oblige. She then spent 3 days in our local mental health crisis unit. Apparently I had been told during my week of orientation not to write her a note. It doesn't matter if you get it word for word exactly what she told you or how you write it - print, cursive, pen or pencil - it's wrong and she can't handle it. I was told a lot of stuff in that week.

Now our orientation book takes about a day and a half to go through with a supervisor (no reading by yourself, no outdated videos) so staff can hear about the basic rules and regulations and policies and procedures that they will be expected to follow, and they can ask questions. It's an orientation, not a training. *Then* we put them in a room with some clients. But there is still a catch… new staff are not allowed to go into the community with a group by themselves for up to 60 days. They go with another experienced staff and their group until they learn more about what they are doing. We assume that they don't know our clients and they don't know what a developmental disability is, much less how to define a behavior or do assessments or any of the fancy things we do… or about the community places we go and how to get there.

We also make them pass a couple of trainings about assaultive behavior as well as first aid and CPR. Let's take the time and show them about the job, then turn them loose. Let them get to know the clients before doing something that could lead to assaultive behaviors where a client or someone else gets hurt. We also have regular staff meetings where we discuss all sorts of issues – regarding staff and clients – together, because none of us are experts in what we are doing. We have found that most staff feel comfortable going out with a group on their own after about 30 days.

They also have 90 days in which to go back to their supervisor and repeat several sections of the basic orientation book. This time it is considered training, but now they have seen and experienced some of what we are talking about. Plus, we now wish them good luck… and, boy, does that make a difference!

Keep in mind here that I said right off the top that I am not an expert in this field. I'm just sharing some things that seem to work pretty well for us. These are things we sit around and worry about instead of worrying about labels.

How did I get off talking about orientation? I was going to tell you about our typical program.

Our brochure says that we provide "social and behavioral skills training for adults with developmental disabilities." Impressive, huh? The people in our community love us and the work we do. They don't actually *know* what it is that we do... but they sure appreciate us for doing it. But you know what I'm talking about. We teach people the skills they need to live independently someday.

Well, no, that's not actually what we do. Say what?! Many people in our own field seem to think that's what we all do in our various day programs across the country; teach people the skills they need to live independently, but we don't. For the most part, we offer people the opportunity to experience and practice as many skills as we can so they can hopefully live comfortably and safely in a supported living arrangement someday.

Supported living is not the same as independent. I went to a conference a couple of years ago where the main theme was about "Independent Living." Every speaker used the phrase "Independent Living." Of course, in the same breath they also used the phrase "With Support." That's another one of those labeling things. Do you mean independent which most people think means mostly on your own with no help, responding appropriately (most of the time) to natural cues, or do you mean with support, which most people think means that someone else is doing some/most stuff for you because you don't always make such good choices for yourself or you just *can't* do things for yourself?

One speaker thrilled the audience with the story of how one of his clients had purchased his own van and now accessed the community independently. Well, the client didn't exactly purchase the van... someone else purchased it and donated it to the client... and he needed a driver to actually drive him around town and operate the wheelchair lift. The crowd roared with excitement. I was certainly happy that this client now had a way to get around town, but I'm not sure I agree that he was doing it "Independently."

But hey, if we want to call that "Independent Living"...

great! That's cool. I'm down with that… I mean, that's hot. I'm up for that. Whatever.

Living at home independently for Bob means living in a house with another adult and two children. These people are labeled as his "family." Bob has very little privacy when he is at home. Most of the rooms in his house are not even equipped with locks to keep out the others. No one ever knocks when they enter the room he is in, he is regularly interrupted by the others in his house when watching his favorite TV shows or sometimes when he is in the bathroom. He is expected to eat meals with the others in his house and he eats what is "for dinner" at the appointed time.

Damned group homes. How can anyone learn to live independently that way?

Oh, wait a minute, I forgot, that's my cousin Bob again. I wonder how many clients in group homes consider their housemates as their "family?" What exactly is so wrong with a group home living arrangement as a supported living arrangement? "Well, the clients have little privacy!" Just like Bob. "But they have to eat what is cooked for them and they eat as a group!" Just like Bob… just like a family does. "Yeah, well… what was the question again?" As long as the clients/residents get to participate in the choices of what to eat and they help out as their skills allow, it really can work.

Are there group homes where client rights are trampled? I'm sure there are, and those places need to be closed down and their staff burned at the stake or some other Type I Punishment (more on that later). Maybe we need to train people how to work in a group home. I don't see or hear much about that.

I absolutely agree that clients have the right to try supported living to see if it works for them, but taking an adult who has lived in a developmental center for their whole life (so far) and immediately putting them in their own house with the right to hire and fire staff as they see fit… that's maybe not always the best thing.

We had a woman enter our program directly from a state developmental center. She had tried community living a couple of other times without success, but she was being given another chance to have a place of her own. I had sort of a chance to meet her before she left the developmental center. The day I drove 250 miles to visit, she was having a "bad day" and I was warned to watch out. I was allowed to say a quick hello as she was laying down taking a nap, before being ushered out of the room... I mean *I* was ushered out, not her. She moved to our town a couple of weeks later into her own apartment, and entered our program a week after that. Boom, bang and it was done.

Marcy (I changed her name... I mean I changed it for the book, not for real), was non-verbal, had some self injurious issues which got worse right after the sudden move, and the local supported living staff who was "transitioning" her to our center assured us that she didn't communicate. We sent her transition staff home and asked them not to come back. She didn't *communicate*? Really? Apparently, her staff thinks "non-verbal" means "can't communicate." Wow! We'll talk about *that* later, too.

I would love to say here that Marcy was a marvelous success story for us. Unfortunately, her mobility issues were more than we could handle at our particular program and she had to leave us. She still lives locally with 24 hour support... at least I hope its support and not staff making all decisions and doing everything for her instead of teaching her to do as much as she can for herself... because she "can't communicate." The last time I was at her apartment, her staff showed me where her gait belt hung and Marcy now knows that when she wants to go for a walk, she gets her leash... excuse me... her gait belt and takes it to her staff. She is seen occasionally going for a walk with her staff holding on to her gait belt so they can control her movements. Controlling movement is not the same as assisting with mobility.

Does that mean that she has "bad" staff or does it mean she has poorly trained support staff? Might it have been better to wait for community placement until there was a better trained and prepared support team ready? Or maybe placement in a group home situation for a while, so she had the opportunity to get used to being with smaller groups of people living with her than the ward she was used to? Yes, she has her own apartment. Her only friends now are the staff who are paid to be with her, but she's in her own apartment and I'm sure somebody feels good about that. I don't know if Marcy feels good about it or not.

Do I think that experience is reflective of all experiences? Of course not. Can we prepare for every possible experience? Of course not. My point is that we also don't need to rush into anything. Unless, of course, all this is driven by economics and not by what is best for individuals. But who am I to suggest such a thing? That would just be silly, wouldn't it.

I recently had a nice conversation with a woman who works for an agency that has, as I understand it, a large campus where people with developmental disabilities can live and receive some training opportunities. Clients are not restricted to the campus by any means. They have access to the community at large with support. She said that in past years, clients could wander the campus freely (without a staff person accompanying them) when they wanted to visit a friend and if someone wanted a haircut, they could stop by the campus beauty shop and get a haircut (unaccompanied by staff) whenever they wanted. Now, they are more community based. This means that if someone wants a haircut, they have to wait until a staff person can accompany them into the community, and if there is a behavioral issue in the beauty shop, the person cutting the hair rushes the job to get the person out of their shop because they are in the business of making money, not providing a training facility for people with behavioral issues.

Am I saying that people with disabilities shouldn't be allowed in the community? No. I am saying that in *some* cases, the person with the behavioral issue *may* have more success if they have a place where they can learn/practice some skills without having people judge them. I think there is room for a number of training options.

We have a woman in our program who lived with her *very* protective mother until she was placed in supported living. Now she makes all her own decisions and can hire and fire her own staff. Of course, she never had the opportunity to make decisions and choices like that before, so she isn't very good at it now. She has a lot of assaultive behaviors at home. We don't see any of those behaviors at our day program. I'd like to say it's because we are so darned good at what we do, but I suspect it's because her staff at home have no training in how to teach her to make choices and she is overwhelmed with her new freedom. We use a principle called "forced choice" to help her learn about making choices at our program. An interim move to a group home with a trained staff, so she could see how other people make choices about their living conditions, may have helped… maybe not. I'm no expert.

I had a staff person freak out over the phrase "forced choice." He was outraged that we were *forcing* these poor people to make choices. He doesn't work for us anymore because (among other things) he never could quite grasp the concept of allowing a client the opportunity to make a choice between two competing alternatives. "Which do you identify with more? This or this?" Then we reinforce them for making a choice. The choices are always socially appropriate choices. Clients make choices every day. "I don't want to do this, so I think I'll bite someone so they leave me alone." Biting is never one of our forced choices.

Think about how you offer choices to clients. Our experience is that if you offer 3 choices to some people, they will either pick the first thing you said because since you said it first, it must be what you want them to choose, or they will pick the third thing you said because it's the one they remember. Too many choices can be as frustrating to some people as not enough choices. Ever been in a restaurant and the menu was so overwhelming you couldn't decide? "I'll have a number C... no wait... make that a number J... oh, look at number S... OK, make it the C... no, wait..."

When *we* do that, we are taking time to make up our minds. When clients do it, they have "difficulty focusing." Three choices; "Do you want to go shopping, go to the museum, or go to the park?" is like that for some people. This principle is not used for everyone... only for people who have never learned to make choices on their own.

"Real life" is that no one is prepared for all clients across the country to immediately enter supported living. I know that move would make us all feel really good about ourselves and we could all have the warm-fuzzies, but no one seems to have thought ahead very far before jumping on the "get everyone out of developmental centers and group homes immediately and into independent living situations" bandwagon.

It also appears that some non-disabled people who have had bad experiences with group homes in the past are now using self directed services as an excuse to bypass group homes and day programs. Give clients money to pick whatever living arrangements they choose... as long as one of the choices isn't a group home or a day program with their friends. All those people are doing is making the same mistake as the people who spend so much time worrying about labels. Quit worrying about where a client might choose to live, and spend some energy providing training to group home staff people. Provide some community outreach to let real estate agents know that people with developmental disabilities have rent money to spend! Don't blame case managers for placing people in open "slots." Those slots may be all that are available because of community stereotypes or limited housing or $500,000 homes that used to cost $110,000. Take advantage of what is available until someone starts training the community.

Does this mean that I am against self directed services? Of course not. People with the skills to do so should absolutely have the right to make their own choices in life. I'm just not sure about limiting their choices once we trust them to make their own choices.

Programs like ours are an interim step. Yes, it is unfortunate that life moves at a slow pace and it will be years before everybody is in supported living, but how about we spend some time on providing a good interim solution while the gears grind and we move steadily, thoughtfully forward instead of rushing into what no one is prepared for?

Interim steps can be good things. I believe I am a much better Site Director because I started out as a lowly line staff. I have been there and done that. I needed the experience to prepare me for what was to come as an all powerful and fearless Site Director. Are you getting the parallel here?

Yes, you in the back with your hand up? What? Isn't it true that most clients never transition out of their day programs? They get placed there and there they stay? Unfortunately, that seems to be true in a number of situations. I still work with clients who have been in our program longer than me. Would I like to see them transition on to supported living placements where they didn't have to attend a day program? Sure, if that's what they want. I don't think seniors should *have* to attend senior centers for socialization with other people "like them" either. But I think many of them choose to do so. Somehow that's OK, but it isn't OK for adults with developmental disabilities to get together in a group with other adults with developmental disabilities for socialization… even if it's their choice. That's also why we frequent public places like coffee shops so our clients get a chance to be around "regular" folks and do "regular" things. Then they can make an informed choice about where they would like to spend their time, and who they would like to spend it with. After all, people with disabilities are really just "regular" folks, too. I know… yet another label.

This has to do with "sub-cultures" in our society. People tend to seek out other people "like them" who have the same interests, the same philosophies, the same backgrounds, the same heath problems, for a support group. But somehow, people with developmental disabilities are not supposed to do that. It's "segregation" if they make that choice.

Apparently, people with developmental disabilities shouldn't "have to" work in sheltered workshops and vocational programs either. I'm not sure why that can't be an option. I have friends who work on assembly lines doing the same repetitive job day after day for low wages. Remember Bob… my cousin, the enclave guy? He doesn't "have to" work there. It's a choice. Maybe our "pre-vocational" programs or "vocational" programs or what ever you call yours aren't meant to teach a client to get a job in the community sorting and shredding paper so much as it is to let them experience what it is like to accept instructions from a supervisor, and to accept responsibility for showing up at the work room on time, and to take a break at break times without needing to be prompted, and to return after breaks without prompting, and so on. Sounds to me like some of the "terrible sheltered workshops and pre-vocational programs" that I have heard about are preparing a person for real life jobs like Bob's after all.

Maybe that's what we are doing in our programs; giving adults who have not had the opportunity to learn those basic skills, or who need more time and instruction to learn those skills, the chance to do so. Remember, a developmental disability doesn't necessarily mean that the person *can't* learn skills. Some folks just learn *differently* than we do and they are learning the basic skills later than most of us did. It's our job to figure out how they *do* learn and give them the opportunity to learn.

Wouldn't it be cool if all clients who work made the same

money as people without disabilities for doing the same job? Yes. I think they should… if they are doing the same job. Performing one task of a job is not the same as doing the same job. We'll talk more about *that* later, too.

Am I saying all vocational programs are well run? No. I'm sure there are lots of inadequately prepared staff with no training or tools available to do their job. Does that mean the whole system is flawed to a point of no return and we should all immediately change what we are doing? I don't think so; no.

Some people like to stress over the fact that in order to even qualify for services, we must focus on a person's deficits and thus begins the labeling process. Yeah, well, I didn't sign up for guitar lessons because I already knew how to play the guitar. I was Strum Challenged – a stigma I shall carry…

Determining a person's baseline is all about discovering what a person can and can't do. If you are *only* focusing on what a person can't do, then you haven't been trained to do your job very well, but it doesn't affect the labeling. We have to call their inability to communicate in a socially acceptable manner *something*. I just don't see how it helps anything to stress over labels and start changing services to fit the new labels.

We have a man in our program who came to us with the label of "Independent" in using the public transit system… until one time when he left program at the end of the day to catch his bus home. He was still there 2 hours later because a new bus driver had pulled up and, noticing that Bill has Down syndrome and wanting to be helpful, asked, "Are you going north?" Bill smiled and answered, "No." The bus drove away, headed north to the town where Bill lives. Bill knew the name of the town, but not the fact that it is north of his day program. So we took some time to focus on his deficit – his inability to identify directions – and taught him to do that. We didn't worry about the label. We just taught him a needed skill.

Does all of this mean that I don't understand that sometimes the words we use can hurt people? Of course not. What it means is that we have to pay attention to the way we use labels. Dismissing a person's ability to participate in community life because of a label of "profound mental retardation" is a sad and hurtful thing. Saying "Well, they're just like children," and then dismissing adults with a disability because you don't understand them is a terrible thing. A statement like, "Yeah, I got a job working with retards trying to change their behavior," is disgusting. Using a label such as "profound mental retardation" as an assessment tool to help us figure out a starting point to help that person become as independent *as they can* is a helpful tool. It's only when we focus on the labels that it really becomes a problem.

I was at a seminar last year selling a curriculum that I wrote, when a presenter at the seminar came up and started looking at the material. She immediately got all up in arms because the material used the word "consumer." She was terribly offended and got even more offended when I said the word out loud. She walked away without even looking at the curriculum because she was so upset at the label of "consumer." This is the silly focus on labeling that I am talking about.

Is the problem with a program is that it's called the "Center for Retarded Citizens," or is it that they don't know what they're doing with clients? If it's a marketing tool to change the name so the community doesn't focus on the stereotype, then yes, by all means, let's change the name. Better yet, let's change the stereotype by participating in the community so the community sees that what they have been told all their lives about people with mental retardation or other conditions isn't necessarily true. If you believe that a name change is going to change the operation of the program, then I think we are wasting some time.

But back to what we do. I was talking about what we do at our center, wasn't I?

At our program, we believe that we are teaching clients some of the skills they will be better able to put into practice when they get into a supported living situation; social and behavioral skills. What the heck are "social and behavioral skills?" There is a basic assumption out there that many adults with developmental disabilities have not mastered the basic communicative skills necessary to interact with non-disabled people on a regular basis. Telling someone that "I need to use the restroom, please" by spitting on them is not considered the social norm. But let's start at the beginning. What the heck is a "developmental disability?" You might be surprised at how many people working in the field don't really know.

Chapter 2 – What Is a Developmental Disability?

The definition of "developmental disability" is described in the U.S. Code at 42 USC 15002 as follows:

Ahem… (I added that),

42 USC Sec. 15002 — Definitions

(8) Developmental disability

(A) In general

The term "developmental disability" means a severe, chronic disability of an individual that:

- is attributable to a mental or physical impairment or combination of mental and physical impairments;
- is manifested before the individual attains age 22;
- is likely to continue indefinitely;
- results in substantial functional limitations in three or more of the following areas of major life activity:
- self care
- receptive and expressive language

- learning
- mobility
- self-direction
- capacity for independent living
- economic self-sufficiency; and
- reflects the individual's need for a combination and sequence of special, interdisciplinary, or generic services, individualized supports, or other forms of assistance that are of lifelong or extended duration and are individually planned and coordinated."

This could include conditions such as Down syndrome (a genetic condition resulting in the development of 24 instead of the usual 23 chromosomes), autism (a complex disability impacting the normal development of the brain in the areas of social interaction and communication skills), cerebral palsy (a condition caused by damage to the brain and characterized by an inability to fully control motor function) and more. Remember that a person can have a condition like cerebral palsy and not have mental retardation, but they may meet the other criteria for adaptive functioning. Don't assume that every person with the diagnosis of Developmental Disability has mental retardation.

You might notice that nowhere in there does it say that adults with any of the listed criteria are child-like or that they should be treated like children. It also doesn't say that they are stupid and can't learn things. It says that they have functional limitations.

We spend most of our time working on Functional Skills Training. How do we determine what a functional skill is? Ask yourself – "If I don't teach this person to do this for themselves, will someone else have to do it for them?" If the answer is, "Yes, if I don't teach this person to determine which public transit bus goes to his/her neighborhood, someone else is going to have to do it for him/her," then it's a functional skill. If the answer is, "No, even if I don't teach this person to count the same 5 plastic thingys repetitively and put them in the same plastic bag over and over, no one else will have to do it for them," and you spend the time teaching them that skill anyway, then you are wasting everyone's time and trouble and shame on you.

Are there programs that do that sort of repetitive nonsense? Yep. Are there programs like ours that give a lot of thought about functional training? Yep. So why is the answer to close down all day programs with group training activities? We provide quite a bit of training to our staff. You might be surprised how little of it is individualized and taught on a 1:1 basis. We figure its information all of our staff can use and we teach it to them in groups. Seems to work for us. Do all clients learn that way? No.

This definition also says that their condition reflects the individual's need for a combination and sequence of special, interdisciplinary, or generic services, individualized supports, or other forms of assistance that are of lifelong or extended duration and are individually planned and coordinated. I take this to mean that there might be lots of kinds of services available so as to fulfill individual needs. Some people might work in "regular" jobs and some people might work in sheltered workshops. Some people might spend their days socializing and having their medical or personal care needs attended to and some might spend all day at home watching TV with their staff friend. Some might attend day programs for social and behavioral skills training. "Individually planned and coordinated" doesn't necessarily mean individually implemented. You can work on many individual skills in a group setting. Really, you can.

We also spend a lot of our time ensuring that our staff treats the adults in our program as adults. Even people with profound (or intense, extensive, pick a label you like) mental retardation deserve to be treated in a chronological age appropriate manner. Just because a 50 year old man displays 5 year old child-like behavior at times does not mean that he *is* 5 years old. He isn't. Trust me on this one. When he smacks you up alongside of the head because he is so frustrated with you not making an effort to find out what he is communicating, you'll know what I mean. Saying things like, "OK, Bob, I'll give you a cookie later if you behave," like you might to a 5 year old, when this 50 year old man is trying desperately to tell you that he needs to pee - right now! - may lead to quite a tantrum, just like a 5 year old might throw when he isn't getting his way. It isn't because he hates you because you have cooties, it's because he hasn't yet learned that there are other ways to ask to use the restroom.

Treating adults with developmental disabilities like a child just lowers everyone's expectations of them… especially of themselves. It should never be said that adults with developmental disabilities prefer toys and games until they have been presented with a variety of chronological age appropriate activities and have been rewarded for their acceptance. This does not mean that coloring crayons must be immediately banned from all day programs nationwide. It means that we offer people a variety of experiences, let them see how other adults their age act around other people, and we reward them (reinforcement, I'll talk more about this later) for their acceptance of the age appropriate behavior. If *all* you are doing is putting out crayons and a piece of paper for clients to scribble all day, then yes, someone should take your crayons away and give you some training on how to engage clients in some functional training activities.

We have an actual school teacher placed at our center to provide adult education classes for our clients and do some other things for us. I watched him outside of my office one day with a (notice the quotes) "low functioning" woman who was about 23 years old. She gets around in a wheelchair and the teacher was trying to teach her to open the door to get outside by pushing the button that opens the door for people with disabilities… or for people with their arms full of stuff. He spent at least 15 minutes explaining to her why it might be important to her to be able to open a door for herself. That's functional training – if she doesn't learn to open the door, someone will have to open it for her. She happily talked about monkeys and chocolate cake. Not once did he slip into childish language – "Oh, come on, Lucy, open the door like a good girl." I was so proud of him. And after about 15 minutes of him explaining to this adult woman and demonstrating a couple of times how it worked, she finally pushed the button and opened the door.

Did she do it just to shut him up or because he was treating her with some dignity for her age? I don't know. I know she opened the door a bunch of times after that and I choose to believe she demonstrated the skill because she was grateful for someone who didn't treat her like a child. It wasn't so much that she didn't know *how* to open the door as she didn't know *why* she should. She's disabled and someone always does it for her.

Why can't we just let clients act like kids if that's what makes them happy? Because most people in our society don't act like a child in stores or at work and our job is to teach them about social norms. That's what will be required to live in community supported living arrangements where they go shopping for their own food, go to the movies, and cash their own paychecks.

We recently had the mother of one of our clients attend a training we provided. We talked about age appropriateness during the training. Afterwards, I mentioned to her that sometimes it is hard for our staff to treat her 25 year old daughter like an adult when she comes to program every day wearing her princess crown and Little Mermaid backpack. The mother was really surprised at that concept. It hadn't really occurred to her before that her baby was now an adult woman and most adult women in our town don't wear princess crowns and Little Mermaid backpacks around town to the store and the bank and post office, etc. Her daughter likes wearing her crown and mom's do what makes their babies happy. Unfortunately, no one was going to take her daughter seriously as an adult until she started dressing and acting like an adult. Mom decided to ask her daughter to wear other kinds of hats once in a while to help her see that people will treat her differently if she looks her chronological age. And we reinforced her choice when she came to program dressed age appropriately. I haven't seen her wear her crown for a while now. It seems she likes the way people treat her without her crown just fine. She made a choice.

Now don't get carried away. We all do silly, childish things once in a while for fun and to be the center of attention. But we don't do them all day every day.

And don't even get me started on "making paper chains."

As long as I am on this track, let me mention Generalization. Will the skills learned in a contrived setting transfer to other settings? Can you learn to buy a soda at McDonald's by practicing in a room in a facility with plastic coins? Now, I know none of you still do that, but we used to. What we learned is that McDonald's absolutely will not accept plastic coins… no matter how much we practiced with them. We also learned that it is really boring and stupid to sit around practicing like that. Now we take actual money and go to McDonald's to buy a soda. We are *so* 21st century!

Also, will the skill of being able to purchase a soda at McDonald's transfer to Denny's? Maybe, maybe not. For some people it isn't the same at all. The stores don't look much the same. In one, you go up to a counter and look above the counter to see what a soda costs and you place your order with the person standing behind the counter ("Do you want fries with that?"). In the other, you sit at a table and wait for a waiter… waitress…waitperson (darned labels!) to bring you a menu, then you order from the waitperson who hovers near your table… if you're lucky.

The good news is, in both places you can interact with other community members and let them get to know you.

Will getting a haircut at a campus beauty shop transfer to a community beauty shop? Maybe. For some clients, after learning some basic behavioral skills in the campus shop; what clippers sound like, how to deal with other people handling your hair, etc., it might be easier to transition to the community shop.

The presumption here is that your staff are letting clients do their own ordering in restaurants and stores to the extent that they are able, and staff aren't just ordering drinks for everyone because it's easier. I mean, have you really, actually talked to your clients (even the non-verbal, "low functioning" people) about how and why they should place their own orders? If it takes a non-verbal client a little longer to place their order, that's OK. What can you do to make it easier for them to be able to place their order? Maybe help them create an icon book with a picture of a coke or of an iced, half-caf, quad, grande, soy, double shot on ice with energy.

We practice nutrition skills at our facility. Will learning to use the gas range at our facility transfer to using the electric stove at home? Depends on the person learning, doesn't it? We take some heat (pardon the pun) sometimes because we teach clients to prepare things like a frozen burrito for lunch. "Oh, that isn't healthy!" You're probably right. There are lots of healthy alternatives to frozen burritos… but a client living in a group home is more likely to have the opportunity to fix a frozen burrito at home on the weekend than prepare a full spaghetti dinner. We also teach them to think about having an apple with that burrito instead of fries.

Does this mean that learning any skill in a facility is worthless? No. Our facility is a great place to meet in the morning, do some socialization with your friends, participate in scheduling activities for the day, and review some curriculum about the skills that you might practice today while out in the community. It's a great place to actually practice using a stove in our kitchen or practice measuring soap and putting it in a washing machine instead of a dryer. We live in a small town and there aren't any community locations where we can practice those sorts of things.

Yes, you with your hand up in the back? What? Can't we practice laundry skills at a community Laundromat? Yes, except for the "funding" thing. It would take a lot of quarters to have several people practice pouring soap in the correct machine, or sorting loads. But yes, you're right, it would be more in line with functional training. People in the community aren't allowed to come here and do their laundry. They go to the Laundromat. Can't we find the money somewhere? Please send all donations to…

And I'll admit this is for our convenience, but when a client is having a bad morning, it is very often better to review emotional curriculum here at our facility than in the middle of K-Mart. Better for whom? I kind of think it is better for both of us. Will talking about emotions at our facility generalize to K-Mart? All I know is that it is much easier to remind someone who is in the middle of throwing a tantrum in K-Mart, "Remember what we talked about this morning about being able to tell me if you are frustrated about something? Well, what's going on?" than it is to try and talk to them about the whole emotions curriculum when they are so upset in the middle of a busy store. What we *don't* do is treat them like a child, "You stop that right now or you won't get your snack!"

Make sure you don't confuse developmental disability with mental illness. Mental illness has its own definition – a group of disorders that cause severe disturbances in thinking, feeling and relating, often resulting in a diminished capability to cope with ordinary daily life. These include conditions such as bipolar disorder, schizophrenia, obsessive compulsive disorder, and post traumatic stress disorder. It is not unusual for our clients to be dual diagnosed; having both a developmental disability and a mental illness. Many also have a physical disability.

In fact, in our program we are seeing more and more people with mental health issues, and our training is in developmental issues. Here again, I see this as a training issue for us instead of a labeling issue about us being a bad system. Instead of closing us down, how about providing some training in mental health issues?

So, beyond the classification definitions (developmental disability/mental illness), remember that a behavior is a behavior is a behavior. You don't look at a behavior and say, "Oh, that was a mental illness assault," or "Clearly, that person is crying because of a developmental disability."

When talking about *any* behaviors, I have to warn you to pay attention to some labels. I know, first I say don't worry about labels, then I say pay attention to labels. Go figure. What *is* the behavior?

For our general purposes, we define a behavior as anything a person does that is observable and measurable. You can see a person hit another person and measure how hard and how many times they struck. You can see someone smile and measure the smile as a wide-mouthed toothy smile or a closed mouth grin. This is called the "Topography" of a behavior. What you cannot see is "happy," or "mad," or "sad," or "frustrated."

What did you see that made you *think* the person was happy or mad? Were they red in the face, clenching their fists and making a growling vocal sound? Does that describe someone who is mad? Or does it describe someone who has gas and is embarrassed to pass gas in front of others so he has learned to display tantrum behaviors such as tipping over the table and throwing chairs so that we will empty the room so no one gets hurt, and he can safely pass his gas? No, I didn't make that one up. This is a case where the label is important.

Mike, the "gassy" guy I just mentioned, had been labeled as "mad" all the time. Just as I started working for our agency someone made the discovery that he wasn't mad, but he was embarrassed and uncomfortable and that's why he displayed the behavior he did.

We talked to him about how gas is a natural phenomenon (causes global warming and everything) and, sure, it can be embarrassing when you do it in front of other people, so how about, "When you feel like passing gas, you tap your fingers on the table. Only you and I will know what that means, and I will ask you if you want to go get a drink of water, and that way you can leave the room and no one will be able to guess why." It took about a year for him to realize that he could ask on his own to go get a drink and be able to leave the room (and pass his gas) and return with no one laughing at him.

The point is, as long as he had been labeled as "mad," no one wanted to be around him and no one was looking for what really might be going on. What did you see that made you *think* he was mad? "He got red in the face, clenched his fists and made a growling vocalization."

When writing our plans, we define the behavior carefully. "Assaultive" is not as defining as "hits others." "Hits others" may not be as defining as "hits others with a closed fist and moderate force." Make sure everyone working with this client understands what behavior we are talking about. "Toileting" is not as defining as "puts objects such as pens and jewelry in the toilet and attempts to flush them." A vague description of "toileting" may mean that they don't know how to wipe their butt. And please… there is no "one plan fits all" for dealing with behaviors.

How intense was the behavior? We developed a standardized set of definitions for describing the intensity of behaviors in our program:

For assaultive behavior, we describe Mild as "they were swinging towards, but either did not make any contact with self or others and it wouldn't have made any marks if contact had been made, or they made light contact (such as 'brushed across') and it did not leave any marks.

Moderate is described as "may cause some redness to self or others, or would have if contact had been made.

We also have descriptors for Severe and Intense intensity. And we have descriptors for aggressive behavior such as yelling, throwing objects, knocking over furniture, etc., and for non-aggressive behaviors such as invading personal space or stealing, getting into other people's belongings, etc.

You may want to consider coming up with your own descriptors for your program. The definitions don't matter as long as you all understand and you all use them consistently.

Other ways to measure behavior are by Cycle – what are the starting and stopping points of an incident? You must define what you consider an "incident." If Bob hits Tom quickly 10 times in a row, is that one incident or ten incidents? It's up to you to define it. Hitting peers with his fists may be the *onset* and the *offset* may be when he stops hitting for 1 or more minutes, no matter how many actual swings/blows there were.

Frequency – how often does a behavior occur? Once a day? Once an hour?

Duration – how long does an incident last? One minute? Five minutes? Rarely does a behavior last "all day" as some staff like to report. There may have been a number of incidents during the day, but an incident doesn't usually last all day. I recently received case notes from two of my staff where one said that an assaultive incident had lasted 1 minute and the other person said it lasted 15 minutes. Turns out that 1 minute was correct. The actual assaultive incident lasted approximately 1 minute. The other person included antecedent and consequence times. We don't include antecedent and consequences in our behavior incident descriptions. A behavioral incident just includes the actual incident as defined. The antecedent and consequence are two other animals altogether. I'll get into that later.

Topography, cycle, frequency, duration, and intensity: now you know how to define and measure a behavior.

I'm sidetracked again, aren't I? I was about to talk about what social and behavioral skills training is.

Chapter 3 – Planning

Before we get into the meat of social and behavioral skills training, you must understand that pretty much all behavior is a form of communication. Let me repeat that – all behavior is a form of communication. There is a reason that Lacy is throwing that tantrum. There is a reason that Bill is ignoring you and won't come out to the transit bus stop with you and your group.

First consider who has behaviors. You do, I do, he does, she does… behaviors occur in people of all age groups, socio-economic segments and hair lengths. However, when working with behaviors in the population we serve, you must take into account the person's disability and how it affects their ability to communicate and how it affects their ability to learn new skills.

I constantly remind our staff that our job is not to stop "bad" behaviors, but to discover what the individual is communicating with this particular behavior, acknowledge the communicative intent ("Oh, *that's* why your keep throwing things at me!") and then figure out what we can teach them to do that is more socially acceptable but still lets them communicate whatever it is that they are saying. I can't possibly over-stress this concept.

The longer you ignore a behavior, hoping that it will go away, the longer you are going to keep getting things thrown at you. Please don't ignore behaviors… either bad or good behaviors. Acknowledge the communicative intent of both. I have said for years that my favorite part of my job is trying to figure out "what is going on inside that person's head?" Always remember that we are responsive to, but not responsible for, a client's behavior. I don't know who first said that, but I like it.

There are lots of ways to discover communicative intent. There are a million assessment forms – ABC, Scatter Plot, Motivational Assessments, etc. – that are very helpful. Another good way is to talk to the individual like an adult and ask them (even if they are non-verbal) to tell you/show you what is going on. You can always ask someone who knows the client better than you do.

You may want to do a Functional Behavioral Assessment. This where we take a look beyond the obvious topography of a behavior and focus on the factors that initiate, sustain, or end the behavior in question. A person who smiles at you and says, "Excuse me, where is the bathroom," and a person who hits you may be communicating the same thing – "I need to go to the bathroom." The *function* of the behavior (why is he doing this?) is to communicate a need to use the bathroom. The *function* is not inappropriate… it's OK to ask for assistance with the bathroom. The *behavior* of hitting to communicate that need *is* inappropriate.

Therefore, it is critical to teach an appropriate replacement behavior that serves the same function as the inappropriate behavior which will also decrease the need for the inappropriate behavior.

I worked with a non-verbal 22 year old gentleman who spent most of his day (this was back in the building with 100 clients) on his knees in a room, playing with toys. Once a day, his toys would become airborne missiles (the behavior). We would clear the room so no one got hurt, then peek in and ask him to please stop throwing things so we could come in and talk to him. "Larry, I need you to talk to me and tell me what

31

you need so I can help you." The fact that he is non-verbal doesn't matter. We talked to him like an adult anyway. We had a list of about ten things memorized. He would eventually stop throwing the objects and let us come in to talk. "Are you too hot? Too cold? Did you get your root beer for lunch? Are you thirsty now? Do you need to go to the restroom?" When we got to the right thing, he would vocalize, "Yeaaaahhhhh" (indicating the function of the behavior). "OK, Larry, the bathroom is right across the hall where it has been for the last 3 years."

Once we split into 3 different facilities with about 30 clients each instead of 100, staff really started working on teaching Larry another way to communicate his need to go to the restroom… or ask for a drink, or whatever. He rarely throws things now. He raises his hand in an approximation of the ASL sign for bathroom (the behavior) when he needs to go (the function of the behavior). And he learned it in a day program. This is going to help him a lot when he gets even more active in community activities. Raising his hand in an approximation of the ASL sign for bathroom is the replacement behavior. It serves the same function as throwing objects, but is a lot safer for all concerned.

This brings up another point – behaviors can communicate a variety of things. In Larry's case, throwing items was a request to use the restroom… and a request to have a drink… and a request to turn the heat down… and seven other requests. You may have to teach a whole series of replacement behaviors to replace the single communicative device the person has been using. Nobody said the job isn't challenging.

We had another young man join our program briefly a couple of years ago. He lived in his own apartment and his home staff would drive him to our facility and would struggle to get him out of the car and into our building. Once inside, he would check out everything, then usually end up hitting someone. Very often he hit a staff person. It didn't matter who he hit, it would get him sent home due to his assaultive behavior.

It seemed pretty clear to us that he was saying, "I don't want to be in your program." He didn't assault people other times and places. He was taken out of our program and his assaultive behavior went away. He has since started at one of our other facilities and he is doing fine. Apparently he likes their program better than ours. My feelings are hurt, but I'll be OK. He had a choice and he exercised his rights. More importantly, we didn't try to stop his "bad behavior" of hitting. We identified what his behavior was communicating and paid attention to what he was saying. I hope the other program is working on teaching him ways to communicate other than hitting.

We have a suspension policy for our program, but we don't use it very much. If the person doesn't understand why they are being sent home, there isn't much point. If the person is doing the behavior in order to *get* sent home, again, there isn't much point. We have to believe that the person understands the concept, and that they don't really want to leave the program right now before we consider using suspension. Suspension is a punishment. I'll talk a lot more about reinforcement and punishment in chapter 4. I don't say that punishment doesn't work or that we never use it (don't get excited, wait for chapter 4), but we would never write suspension into a plan as a way to get Bob to stop doing a behavior. We would work on a replacement behavior... what would we like the Bob to do instead of the behavior that resulted in suspension? We might use suspension to *manage a behavior* until the replacement behavior is learned.

Back to why we do assessments. We are currently working with a woman who spends up to an hour... or 5... in the restroom. She has seen a doctor and there is no apparent medical reason for her to be in there that long. We are still trying to determine what she is telling us by being in there. "I need some private time to work out my problems... I don't want to go to town today... I don't like the staff person I am with..." She does this at home, too, or we might believe she is saying, "I don't want to be at program." She is a verbal person, but she chooses to communicate by her bathroom behavior for some reason.

We had written this great plan for her to exit the restroom within 10 minutes. Then we looked at the plan again. Gee, I sometimes spend more than 10 minutes in the bathroom... especially the older I get or if it's a really good interview in Playboy this month. Why would we work on a plan for her to exit a restroom in 10 minutes? How about exiting a restroom when she is finished with her business? How about finding out why she is in there and then coming up with a plan to replace that behavior? Part of the plan is assessing the conditions prior to her spending so much time in there. She doesn't do it every time, or only on Wednesdays, or only when it is raining. We'll gather enough data to see a pattern eventually. Patience, Grasshopper.

An important point here is that we are not trying to stop her "bad behavior" of spending too long in the restroom. We *are* trying to manage the behavior while we figure out what the communicative intent of the behavior is, then we can teach her a replacement behavior. Once we discover what she is saying, it will be up to us to teach her another way to say the same thing in a way that doesn't hold up groups in the community waiting for her to come out of the bathroom.

It is very easy to say, "Well, they're just doing it for the attention." Maybe. Social attention may be the reason. Or maybe not. If that is your assumption, then you obviously aren't doing any assessments to discover the function of the behavior. It might be interesting for you to spend a little time to try and figure out why they *really* are doing the behavior. You might be surprised.

This brings me to writing plans. I would love to say that we are experts at writing plans, but I guess the story I just told sort of negates that. All I can say is that we are spending a lot more time thinking about our plans now than we used to. Person Centered Planning wasn't really in effect when I started in this business. We used to gather for an Individual Service Plan (ISP) meeting - ISP, IEP, IPP, IP, choose one you like, they're all about the same no matter what we call them - and announce things like, "Susan, you seem to spend a lot of time in our paper shredding room, so let's give you a Long Range Goal of 'increasing your vocational skills', and let's give you an Objective of 'participating in paper shredding twice per week'. And our plan to teach you that will be for staff to track when you do it. Next!"

I am so glad that we have finally decided that all people with developmental disabilities don't necessarily need to know how to "set the table." That used to be a popular one. This is where Person Centered Planning starts – "Bob, dream a little… what would you like for someday in your life? What changes would you make to your life if you could do or have anything?"

We've gotten some really interesting responses. One of my favorites was the man who said that he wanted to be an airplane pilot. His mother happened to be attending the meeting and she turned to her son and said, "Oh, Jim, that's just silly." We had to politely tell her to be quiet and let Jim talk. We asked him what he thought that meant, and he knew; sit up front and drive the airplane. So that's what we wrote down.

It doesn't matter to us if we think it is realistic or not. It's not my job to stomp on anyone's dream. What if my mother had told me as a child that I could never be the Site Director of a poorly funded private non-profit social services program? I would have been crushed.

My all time favorite was Lisa, who said, "I want to be a topless dancer!" All righty, then. And she knew exactly what that meant; work at the Go-Go Club (the name has been changed to protect the innocent), take off her shirt and "shake 'em for the guys." We wrote that one down as being an exotic dancer.

The real challenge becomes; what in the world are we going to teach Lisa so that she might be a topless dancer someday? "Always start with the top button. OK, everyone, undo your top button, watch me, now, in time with the music…"

Actually we talked to her about being on stage, and how people on stage often wear stage make-up and maybe she might like to learn how to wash her face in order to prepare for putting on the make-up. She liked that idea just fine and she stayed with our program for several months. That was an improvement over the several weeks she usually spent before taking off for a while. She came because we were offering something that she was interested in learning.

We often find that when asked about someday in their future, the client says something like, "I want to go to K-Mart with Bob today." There are lots of clients who have trouble with the concept of thinking very far ahead. Their idea of planning is "what are we going to do *next?*" That's OK. Just talk to the client and help them try to think bigger.

You've heard the old thing about writing SMART plans?

S – specific.
M – measurable.
A – action oriented.
R – realistic.
T – time limited.

There's actually a lot to be said for that. We insist that the Objective and the plan follow those steps.

The Long Range Goal is what the person wants someday - the Objective is what we are going to work on at our facility to help them in the direction of their Goal. Some people call Objectives "Short Term Goals." The label doesn't matter. It's the content that's important. I think it's unlikely that someone would have a Long Range Goal of "Doing their own laundry." Really? Someone said that their life-long dream is to do laundry? If that's what they said, then by all means, write it down…

or marry them or something. But probably, their dream is something like "to live in an apartment of my own."

How many Long Range Goals are appropriate? It depends. How many dreams does the person have? You can have a Long Range Goal with no Objectives currently assigned to it.

Specific – what is the skill that the individual wants/needs to work on? Let me emphasize that... what is *the skill* that the individual wants to or needs to work on? This will become an Objective in their plan. What skill(s) do they need to live on their own? Crossing the street? That's a whole series of skills. Now, here's the hard part. You have to look at those nasty old deficits. Why can't the person cross the street safely now? What barrier prevents them from doing it? "They wander out of the crosswalks into traffic." OK, then, there's a skill to work on. Why can't Bob live on his own now? "He can't do his laundry and would always be wearing dirty, stinky clothes." Why can't he do his laundry? Does he know how to sort clothes for washing? Is that *the skill* he needs to learn before learning the rest of the skills which make up "doing his laundry"... which will contribute to his living on his own someday?

Be careful of clothing issues. Wearing stinky clothes is a right that some people heartily embrace in our community. You can certainly talk to a person about social awareness, but we can't make a person wear clean clothes unless it is a health or safety issue. And even then we can't *make* them wear clean clothes. We *can* restrict their access to our program for health and safety reasons.

And be careful on your wording so you aren't working on stopping some "bad" behavior. "Tina will refrain from throwing a tantrum in the store." What do you want her to do instead? Why is she throwing tantrums? "Tina will be able to use the ASL sign for restroom." I'd throw a tantrum too if no one helped me/let me go to the bathroom when I needed. And does it need to be the actual ASL sign, or will an adaptation suffice?

You must give serious thought to the functionality of an ISP Objective as well as how realistic is it for staff to teach this skill in a group setting, as well as your reasonable expectations of the client's ability to learn the skill. If Bob regularly walks to the store in the evenings from his group home, why are we still working on street crossing skills as part of a structured plan? It might be to maintain those skills... or it might just be annoying to Bob because he already has those skills.

How many Objectives are appropriate for a client? Again, it depends on the client. If they have a serious behavioral issue that prevents them from accomplishing most things, then a single Objective dealing with the behavior is probably enough for now. We probably aren't going to teach Bob to stay within the crosswalk lines if he takes off running randomly every time we approach a street corner. Let's work on the running behavior first.

Consider that there are generally three reasons for an Objective: the client needs to acquire a completely new skill; the client needs practice to master a skill; the client has a behavioral issue to overcome.

Objective statements need to be about a specific skill or a specific sequence of skills. Keep asking yourself, "What is *the skill* the client will be working on?" "Bob will follow a 3 step plan to do his laundry," isn't much of a statement. Do you mean, "Bob will be able to complete the sequence of sorting clothes in to white and colored piles, load the appropriate pile into the washer and make the correct setting to wash"? Or does Bob have difficulty with sequences and needs to get one step down first – "Bob will be able to sort a load of laundry into white and colored piles." This is not the same as "Bob will be able to get laundry ready to wash." "Bob will be able to measure one full cup of liquids." This is not the same as "Bob will be able to measure ingredients." "Bob will be able to check the oil level on a lawnmower for engine maintenance." This is not the same as "Bob will be able to maintain a lawnmower." What is *the skill?*

Measurable – how are you going to measure progress or lack of it? This is what we call Criteria. Generally we measure the speed, accuracy, quality, or frequency of an Objective. The first thing you must do is define "what is success?" for this Objective.

Objective statement: Bob will be able to safely maneuver across a crosswalk in the allotted time limit.

What is success? Getting across the street while the light is green so he doesn't get hit by a car.

Criteria: Speed - How fast can Bob accomplish the task? "Maneuvering to the opposite curb before the light turns red."

Objective statement: Bob will be able to leave a clear message on an answering machine when he calls home for assistance.

Accuracy – Did he get it complete and right? "Correctly identifying the name of the town and three distinguishing features of his surroundings."

Objective statement: Bob will choose to say "excuse me" after he burps or passes gas in public.

Quality – "Immediately saying 'excuse me' in a voice loud enough to be heard by those possibly offended." Saying it loudly enough for everyone in the restaurant to hear would be outside the boundaries of our Quality assessment... unless he burped loudly enough for everyone in the restaurant to be offended... but we won't go there.

Objective statement: Bob will choose to answer yes or no using words.

Frequency – How frequently does the person do the task? "At least 3 clear yes or no verbal responses per day."

Frequency is often used another way in behavioral Objectives. "Bob will choose to respect personal boundaries by only touching others with their consent." Criteria: "Reducing the number of incidents to 3 times per day (or by 10% or whatever number you decide on)." I know, this seems counter intuitive – we are measuring success by reducing the number of incidents of a "bad behavior?" Counting only the number of successes of an Objective such as "Bob will choose to respect personal boundaries by only touching others with their consent," may be misleading. He may be successfully touching with consent 10 times per day now... and is up to touching inappropriately 30 times per day! You will probably want to count both ways on your tracking sheets, but a successful measurement of a reduction in inappropriate touching tells you that he is only touching with consent more often, and that's what our Objective statement asked for... only touching with consent, which is the replacement behavior for touching all the time whether people want to be touched or not. If we are successful at teaching the replacement behavior, then the incidents of inappropriate behavior should automatically be reduced. Should... maybe... oughta. Keep in mind that this is an introductory sample and not an explanation of how all behavioral criteria works. This is just to get you thinking.

Be wary of Criteria statements such as, "By flushing the toilet when he is finished." Does this mean that the actual skill we should be working on is his ability or choice to flush the toilet?

If you can't measure it, take another look at your Objective statement. Speed, quality, accuracy or frequency are measurements.

This is a good place to talk about Baselines, too. What is the person's current skill level or usual state of behavior? What are you going to measure success against? Statements to the effect that "Bob said he wants to learn to wash his hands," doesn't tell us anything about how good he is at washing his hands right now. "Bob requires a direct verbal prompt to lather his hands with soap," is a baseline.

"Bob properly secures the caps on his oil paints 50% of the time when he is finished with projects," is a baseline. "Bob wants to (or should or needs to) take care of his supplies," is not a baseline.

The only way to establish a baseline is to look at tracking sheets, or to complete appropriate assessments and get some data about the client which includes some direct observation.

Action oriented – who is going to do what, when? Specifically. Be careful not to make it the staff person's plan. What is the client going to do as well as the staff? Here are some things you might want to consider:

What instructional process will staff use to teach this skill? A prompting hierarchy? Shaping? Chaining? What is this person's individualized prompting hierarchy and what might some examples of the prompts look/sound like? For example, "When staff says, "Where does the cup go?" they are effectively using an Indirect Verbal prompt." This isn't the only way to word the prompt, but it gives staff an idea of the type of statement that may work. I'll talk more about prompting hierarchies in a bit. But let staff know so that everyone uses the same hierarchy the same way with the client. "Put the cup in the left side of the cabinet," is an effective Direct Verbal prompt.

What is the instructional cue staff will use to let the client know that we are working on the skill now? Or are we just going to surprise them and wonder why they didn't respond? "Bob, let's work on your street crossing skill at the next corner."

Functionality. Why are we trying to teach this skill to this person? It might be because they want to learn it and they will get a sense of pride for achieving the skill, or it may be that if they don't learn it, someone will have to do it for them. Are you really teaching a person to count change so they can make a purchase using the exact change? How often do *you* buy things with exact change? Are you teaching the skill so the client can tell if a store clerk is ripping them off? That's more likely.

Are there any specific materials (SNAP Curriculum or such) that are available for staff to reference? What activities might the client and staff engage in to help them learn the skill? "Bob will engage in discussions with his peers and staff regarding the 'Street Safety' curriculum. Bob will stop at corners, including driveways and alleys, look both directions and make a verbal determination if it is safe to cross before stepping off the curb." This is not the *only* way to teach Bob safe crossing skills, it's just a good way. We hire a lot of inexperienced staff at our program who need some direction on how to teach skills.

Frequency and Duration. How often should the client be offered the opportunity to work on this skill? One trial per week? Three trials a day? And for how long each time if that's important. A "trial" includes giving the instructional cue and following through with the complete prompting hierarchy or whatever instructional process you are using.

Reinforcers. What specific reinforcers should staff use with this Objective? If a material reinforcer is going to be used, who is going to deliver it and when? If there is a specific phrase that the client responds to as a social reinforcer, what is it? What reinforcement schedule is the client on? Continuous - reinforce every time the client is successful? Or Intermittent - every third time (for example) they are successful? Think about fading reinforcers over time.

Measurement and Continuity. What happens if Bob refuses to work on this skill? Or if he learns it faster than you expected? It is perfectly acceptable to make adjustments to a plan as you go along. Don't lock the client and yourself into a plan that doesn't work.

Realistic – Long Range Goals do not have to be realistic to us… but the specific Objective does. You can't teach someone computer skills if there isn't a computer available to work on. You can't attend the Thursday Adult Education reading class if you don't attend on Thursdays. You can't teach a person to shred paper if they really don't want to learn to shred paper. You can't teach them to look for an apartment if they aren't motivated to look for an apartment. And can we teach motivation?

Time limited – When is this going to be done? Is there an end date in sight? We aren't just going to work on this forever, are we? What happens when the time is up? What if they still don't have the skill? What if they can do it sooner than you guessed? Are we going to keep working on it and have staff faithfully track each day's progress just because we said we thought it would take Bob a year to learn a skill but he learned it in six months?

I could write a whole book about writing plans. In fact, I *did* write a book about writing plans. It's called Individual Service Plan Guidelines. I'll tell you where you can get a copy at the end of this book.

I recently read a book where a gentleman was decrying

the "fix the problem" approach of our current national system. He believes that we should find creative "work arounds." Does this mean that instead of teaching Bill about north and south, we should work around it and have him take a taxi where the driver won't ask him if he is going north like the bus driver did? There, we got around that nasty old problem!

Don't get excited here. This is certainly not the only way to write plans. It's a good way that works for clients and staff in our program, but all of this information is just to get you thinking about how you write your plans. You'll notice that I haven't mentioned formats at all. It's the content that is really important, not how it's laid out.

But I was about to tell you what I mean about the social and behavioral skills training we do at our program, wasn't I?

Chapter 4 – Reinforcement

I just remembered something: earlier I briefly mentioned Replacement Skills… just in case someone reading this still isn't sure what I mean, you have to remember that our job is not to stop "bad" behaviors. We have to discover what the behavior is communicating, acknowledge the communicative intent, and then find a replacement behavior which allows the person to communicate the same need in a socially acceptable way. What would be more socially appropriate (and possibly safer) for them to do *instead* that still lets them tell me what they need to tell me?

Yes, I know I'm repeating myself. It's important.

Please don't skip this section. If we just stop a person from doing their "bad" behavior, how are they supposed to tell us what they need or want? Instead of thinking, "Why would s/he *do* that?" think instead, "Why *would* s/he do that?" I know it's a subtle difference, but it's an important one. You can never take behaviors personally.

If Tom's way of saying, "I need to use the restroom," is to throw something at you, how will he tell you he needs to go when you stop him from throwing things? Or is he supposed to just pee his pants? A replacement behavior might be to use the ASL sign for restroom… or to whistle or something other than throwing things.

If Barbara's behavior is to ignore a staff person that she

really doesn't want to be with, and we teach her to stop ignoring people, how will she tell us that she doesn't like that staff person? Spit on them? Maybe she could look through some pictures of staff and point to whom she does want to be with. That would be a replacement behavior.

Check your own thinking process – what do we want Bob to do? "We want him to stop biting people." I understand, but what is it that we want him to do? "We want him to be less assaultive." OK, let me phrase it another way, what does Bob want? "He wants a snack out of his lunch and he bites when he doesn't get it." What would you rather Bob do instead of biting you when he doesn't get his snack? "I'd rather he didn't bite me." But then how can Bob express his frustration when he doesn't get his snack? "He could squeeze the heck out of a pillow or something." Ah, sounds like we just came up with a possible replacement behavior.

You have to be very careful when extincting behaviors. OK, I couldn't help myself. I knew the term and I just had to use it. Extinction is a way of eliminating undesired behaviors by withholding a previously available consequence. Or another way of saying it is, "it's the stopping of positive reinforcers that have been maintaining inappropriate behavior."

If yesterday everyone laughed at Tom's jokes which interrupted your activity, today you would ask everyone not to laugh at him when he tells a joke. When he tells his joke and he doesn't get the laughter he got yesterday, he will be less likely to tell another joke during the activity. That is a pretty simplified explanation, but I felt moved to explain.

But, if you extinct Tom's joke telling behavior, unless you pair it with a replacement behavior, he is probably going to find another way to get his attention and you may not like what he comes up with.

Of course, talking about extinction leads into a discussion of Reinforcement and Punishment... keeping in mind that we are giving simple explanations to introduce basic concepts.

Reinforcement, basically, is anything that happens following a behavior that increases the chances of the behavior occurring again in the future. Reinforcement is used to *increase* a behavior.

And just in case you thought we couldn't possibly make a simple concept like that confusing, there are Positive and Negative reinforcements. Positive reinforcement means that you add a desired stimulus (like verbal praise) in order to increase a behavior. "Good job, Bob!" is probably the most overused phrase in social services... but if it is effective for a client, continue using it!

Negative reinforcement means that you remove a disliked stimulus (like the annoying bell that goes off until you put on your seatbelt) in order to increase a behavior. You increase your behavior of buckling up in order to remove the disliked stimulus of the bell. It would be pretty unusual to see a plan specifying that negative reinforcement should be used when teaching Bob to rinse his hands after soaping and lathering them ... "when Bob rinses his hands, staff will stop ringing the annoying bell"... but at least now you know what it is.

Remember that positive reinforcement does not refer to how nicely you say something to a client (and you would be surprised how many people think that's what it means) – it's about adding a desired stimulus to increase a behavior. Both positive and negative reinforcement are used to *increase* behavior. If it has the word reinforcement in it, it's meant to increase a behavior.

Punishment, on the other hand, is anything that follows a behavior that decreases the chances of that behavior occurring again in the future. Punishment is used to *decrease* a behavior.

And wouldn't you know, there are different types of punishment. Type I means that you add an undesired stimulus (like a traffic ticket) to decrease the behavior and Type II means that you remove a desired stimulus (I'm going to turn off the music you chose because you are...) to decrease a behavior. Remember the mention of a suspension policy earlier? Suspension is a Type II punishment. You are removing a desired stimulus of participating in program in order to decrease a behavior. Again, this is assuming that they didn't do the behavior in order to get out of having to be at your program in which case your Type II punishment just became a Positive Reinforcement to increase their hitting behavior. Yeah, this stuff can be tricky.

Isolating someone is a form of punishment. You are isolating them in order to decrease a behavior. "Put on your dunce cap and sit in the corner by yourself. Maybe you'll think twice before you do that again." It is also considered a form of restraint if you put them in a room by themselves and don't let them out until they "calm down." This is called "seclusion." Letting a person remove themselves from a situation so they can calm themself is not the same thing. I'm always a little wary of "time out rooms."

Let me state right here – you will never see punishment written into any treatment plan in any program I run. I am describing punishment here so you will understand what it is and be able to recognize it when you use it. I am not saying that using punishment doesn't work. If I yell at someone to get them to stop twisting my nose in a new and unusual direction, I am punishing them to get them to immediately decrease the behavior of breaking my nose. I will attempt to change the behavior with positive reinforcement of a replacement behavior which lets them communicate the same message in a socially acceptable and pain free manner, and *that* will be in our treatment plan.

Any time you forcibly prevent a person from moving about, you are restraining them. This includes grabbing someone to prevent them from going behind a counter in a store because it might be embarrassing to you. Restraint is a violation of a person's rights. This is serious stuff. You sure can identify possible consequences – "Bob, if we don't go back on the other side of the counter, this nice waitress might call the police." And if she *does* call the police, that's a natural consequence of that type of behavior. Safety issues may be another matter. You may have to restrain a person to prevent them from seriously injuring themselves or another person. Check your agency policy!

Locking a person's wheelchair brakes to keep them from wandering off is a restraint, too, unless the person can reach down and unlock the brakes any time they want to move.

Don't confuse restraint with physical prompting. Physical prompts are a hands-on principle used to encourage a person to do something such as using a computer mouse, or to hold a book, or eat their own lunch. Assisting someone into place in front of the sink to brush their teeth is a physical prompt. We might use a physical prompt to redirect a person's direction if they are headed into a street with busy traffic. Physical restraint is also hands-on, but with a prompt, you are willing to let go if they pull away. In a restraint, you latch on tighter when they pull away to prevent them from doing something or going someplace.

I had a staff assure me once that a client was "independently" throwing away her trash after eating lunch. I was surprised to hear this. "Oh, yes," staff said, "all we have to do is move the trash can next to her after she eats, and she throws away her trash every time!" OK. Except that moving the trash can into place for her is a physical prompt.

Back to reinforcement; there are categories of reinforcers:

Primary reinforcers are things that are reinforcing to pretty much all of us – food, drink, shelter, warmth. They also include natural things like if you take a shower and people stand next to you without cringing and muttering under their breath. We all like people not cringing and muttering when they stand next to us. And yes, I know, there are exceptions to everything.

Secondary reinforcers are things we will work to earn. Verbal praise, pats on the back, and stars on a chart are all types of things we might work to earn. Your paycheck is a secondary reinforcer. Your paycheck may not be reinforcing to everyone (if you work in social services, you know what I'm talking about), but you will work to receive it.

Sub-categories of secondary reinforcers include:

Social reinforcers - come from other people. Hugs, smiles, pats on the back, high fives, and verbal praise are all social reinforcers. These can generally be used in any setting and can be given multiple times per day.

Material reinforcers - includes objects that a person may enjoy such as a certificate of appreciation, or an award ribbon, a gift certificate, stickers, etc. Remember, it may not be practical to give a certificate of achievement every time Bob successfully completes washing his hands throughout the day. You *can* give him a certificate if he successfully washes his hands 100% of the time for a whole week.

Activity reinforcers - are things a person enjoys doing such as playing a computer game as a reinforcer for working on a specific computer skill, or the opportunity to go shopping, choosing the background music for an activity, etc. As with material reinforcers, activity reinforcers are appropriate for people who do not need immediate reinforcement for every successful completion of a task. This is called a delayed reinforcer.

Token reinforcers - are something tangible, like a coupon, which is exchanged later for a social, material or activity reinforcer. Your paycheck is a token reinforcer. You work to receive a coupon (your check) which you exchange later for more tokens (money) that you exchange for stuff you really want… like medical care and gasoline, and rent… gee, I'm getting depressed. Make sure the client understands the concept of things like "funny money" as a token reinforcer. If they believe that WalMart accepts "funny money" because you gave it to them, then there could be a problem.

Give a lot of thought to the behavior you are reinforcing. Are you reinforcing John "not throwing things" or are you reinforcing his "using an ASL sign to let people know he needs to use the restroom?" Pay attention to *when* you reinforce some things, too. If John uses his sign then wipes his nose before you get around to reinforcing him, he may take the reinforcer for wiping his nose. "Oh, you like that? Well, I can dig really deep. Watch this!" You might wait until he is focused on the sign again before delivering the reinforcer. This is called a "limited hold."

Labeling reinforcement is very beneficial, also. What? Labeling is good? What are you, crazy? "John, thank you for using the ASL sign," lets him know exactly what he did right. "Tom, good job looking both ways before stepping off the curb." "Mary, you should be proud of yourself for not hitting Ralph when he took your book."

Reinforcers must be individualized. Let me repeat that – reinforcers must be individualized. Giving everyone in a group a big thumbs up when John does his replacement behavior may not mean much to John. In fact, a thumbs up may be another kind of sign to him altogether. You have to find out what is reinforcing to each individual. We work with a woman who absolutely hates any form of group recognition. If she gets an award for something, she wants it given in private. That's OK, as long as it means something to her and it reinforces (increases) her behavior.

There is a man in our program who needs to hear lavish praise. Just saying, "Good job, Rick," doesn't cut it with him. He wants to hear something like, "Wowza! Way to go Rick. That was so cool! Great job staying in the crosswalk, man." Reinforcers must be individualized.

Let me offer a caution about reinforcers. Be careful about using food as a reinforcer. Very often food seeking becomes an issue. What you chose as a reinforcer becomes a whole new behavior in itself. And what happens if you run out of M&M's in the middle of the day? It isn't against the law or anything, I'm just saying be careful.

And do not use reinforcers as a bribe for a behavior. Reinforcers must be earned by the client. "C'mon Bob, if you stop yelling, I'll take you out for coffee," is not a reinforcer for Bob using a replacement behavior for his yelling behavior. I guess you could say that a bribe is a reinforcer to increase a person's manipulative behavior. That's a bit counter-productive.

Think about fading reinforcement sometime. Our goal is not to make Alice dependent on hearing our praise when she washes her hands. We want her to fade to a natural reinforcer – Alice sees that her hands are dirty, so she washes her hands in order not to get jelly on her art project. She washes her hands, her art work stays clean. Clean art work is the natural reinforcer.

This reminds me – we are not after compliance when working with clients. Our goal is not to get a client to make a good choice only when we tell them to. Yes, you with your hand up in the back? What? Don't we want compliance when someone is standing in the middle of a busy street? Yes. Safety issues are almost always the exception to everything I say. But why were they standing in the middle of the street in the first place?

Instead of compliance, I think we are after a person to be assertive and make good choices. "Hmmm, there are a bunch of cars coming. I think I'll wait until it's clear before crossing the street."

Have you ever heard of "prompt dependence?" That's where a client waits for us to prompt them to do something... like take a break at break time, or get a drink of water, or take a medication at the proper time. We have a woman in our agency's vocational program who recently complained to a staff person that she didn't get her break that afternoon.

When asked what time break time is, she said, "Two o'clock."

How long does break last?

"Fifteen minutes."

Is it that way every day?

"Yep."

Then why didn't you take a break?

"No one told me to."

Do you know why we don't repeat prompts when using a prompting hierarchy? We don't want to teach Jim to get out the way of that speeding bus after every third prompt - "Jim, look out for that speeding bus! Jim, look out for that speeding bus! Jim, look out... oh, darn. That'll be a bunch of paperwork..." - or to wash his hands after every third prompt, or whatever. Until he learns to do those things with a natural cue, we want him to do it with the least restrictive prompt on his "individualized" prompting hierarchy. Please note the word "individualized" in case you missed it.

Did any of you ever used to count the number of prompts on your tracking sheets? We did. That was silly. I presume everyone knows that it is OK to stop doing silly things. Oh, wait... "silly" is a label, isn't it? You only give each prompt once if you are using the prompting hierarchy correctly anyway.

Labels aside, we must be able to change our programs as necessary. I truly don't believe there is anything inherently wrong with day programs as a system, as long as we get the necessary training to do the job correctly and we are willing and able to change and adapt to what works for our clients. As I said before, in order to fill everyone's needs, there needs to be a variety of services available to choose from. Just leaping into a whole new system sounds exciting, but may not be necessarily practical.

Sticking with things because "that's the way we've always done them" doesn't make much sense either. Do you suppose there's a middle ground?

When I wore my fireman label with the U.S. Forest Service, I designed a new hose pack for carrying and distributing hose lines up steep hills. My supervisor at the time wouldn't acknowledge the design because, "We didn't use anything like that when I worked for the State fire service, harrumph, harrumph." OK, I wasn't suggesting that we change the entire way we fight fires. The basic system of fire fighting worked just fine. All I suggested was a small change to improve what we were doing on the ground. We went ahead and used it anyway because it worked.

It's the same with what we are doing here. I'm not suggesting that we stick with what we have always done in day programs because it's what we have always done. In fact, I often ask my staff to question why we do things. I don't want us to get stuck in a rut. I also don't think we need to scrap everything and start over. We don't even all need to do everything exactly the same. Our clients aren't all exactly the same. We can probably just make a few adjustments here and there and keep providing a variety of services. It just drives me nuts when people say that changes are needed, and then they stop there. That's why I wrote a new orientation book for our program. It's pretty much why I wrote this book, too. I think some changes are needed and here are some ways to look at making those changes.

There is an axiom in advertising that says, "Never list a feature without listing a benefit." "This is a great widget. It has a slicer-dicer-curler (the feature) that will save you time and money (the benefit)!" I feel the same way about talking about changing our systems of providing service. "This is a great idea, here's why, and here's a way you can make it happen!" Too many people stop at "This is a terrible idea! It needs to change!"

I also had a problem with hiring 20 year old inexperienced staff and telling them, "Talk to Marsha about emotions, today." What does that mean, exactly – talk to her about emotions? How is this 20 year old inexperienced staff person supposed to know how to talk to adults with developmental disabilities about emotions… something they may not be in full control of in their own life yet? I knew I could complain about it or I could do something about it.

I researched the internet for curriculum designed to talk

with adults with developmental disabilities about a wide range of issues. I found nothing that fit our needs. At that point I could either sit and complain privately or I could write a book and complain about it publicly, or I could write a curriculum. I spent nearly 3 years writing the Specific Natural Activity Program (SNAP) Curriculum.

The SNAP Curriculum is designed for staff to facilitate discussion and review with clients about all kinds of issues. There are over 200 topics covered in the Community Resources, Independent Living Skills, Vocational, and Leisure domains. Each individual curriculum comes from an actual client ISP. For a long time I could tell you the name of the individual I had in mind when I wrote each piece (OK, I couldn't really tell you their names because of confidentiality, but you know what I mean).

Our staff now uses this material on a daily basis. For the most part, it is designed to be used in the community where the skills will be used. It isn't a lecture series and it isn't intended for a client to read and "get it."

Now it doesn't matter if we hire inexperienced staff or which staff works with which client today because all staff will be using the same base of information when talking to clients. Every person will add their own life experience to the discussion, but the base message is the same. And we have discovered that continuity of message really makes a difference.

I also initiated and helped write a series of trainings for staff in the basic concepts of behavior analysis. We call it: Behavior Analysis Skills – Introductory Course (BASIC Training). Online trainings are fine, but there's nothing quite like listening to an actual person who has been there and done that and being able to ask questions, and hear stories from other participants. It gives our staff some continuity in basic skills. We have opened the training up to people from other agencies, school teachers, etc. and they are turning out to be quite popular (the trainings, not the people).

My point? Quit complaining and do something productive! You don't have to write a book. Just look at what changes you might make in your agency to provide better services to clients.

Speaking of continuity, wouldn't it be great if a person's ISP carried over from program to home? How often have we taught a client that tomatoes are green, only to have their care provider pick them up and tell them that tomatoes are red. (We live on a cold, foggy coast and we think tomatoes are *supposed* to be green little hard things). Joking aside, continuity should be carried through beyond a day program or a care home or supported living arrangement. Those should be and's instead of or's.

We had a gentleman in our program who used to draw his hands up inside of his sleeves. This was a problem when he tried to pick up anything. We had this great plan that included the phrase, "Hands out, please," and he responded pretty well to it… but not consistently. Then we found out that the staff at his group home were working on the same behavior, but they were using a different phrase. How confusing was that for the client? They liked the phrase we were using and started using the same phrase at home. His behavior changed rather quickly after that and he didn't drop nearly as many items.

Don't get the wrong idea, we weren't trying to get him to completely stop drawing his hands up… just leave his hands out when he was trying to pick up something or open a door, etc. Having his hands drawn up wasn't a "bad" behavior that we needed to stop.

Masturbation isn't necessarily a "bad" behavior that we need to stop, either. The time and location can sure be inappropriate, though.

I've read a lot lately about the problem of programs like ours trying to "manage behavior." Maybe I read too much. But you know what? Despite our best efforts to provide positive, meaningful programming options, the people we work with sometimes insist on displaying severe behavior problems that present a potential threat to themselves, to others, and to property. It's like, sometimes, they didn't read their plan. So yes, sometimes we attempt to manage behavior until positive programming has time to work. We have labeled these principles "Principles of Behavior Management."

For the most part, these behavior management principles are just common sense. They probably didn't really need years and years of intense behavioral study by someone with the letters PhD after their name, and colorful charts and graphs, in order to figure them out.

I'm talking about principles such as removing seductive objects. We have a man in our program who is obsessed with children's toys – to the point of taking toys out of a child's hands in the community – which really freaks out some mothers – or entering toy stores and spending the rest of the day opening packaging – which really freaks out some clerks. Sometimes, if Richard is headed for the public transit stop, but he walks by a toy store, he is going to miss the bus. So we remove the seductive object. Don't walk by the toy store on the way to the bus stop. Walk around the parking lot the other way if necessary. This doesn't mean we never take him to toy stores. We just avoid them when we are trying to catch the bus.

Relocate people. Don't sit people next to each other if you know they don't like each other. I know this sounds dumb, but I've seen it happen.

Remove unnecessary demands and requests. What are unnecessary demands and requests? The ones that cause clients to become assaultive. I don't like it when someone demands compliance from me. It kind of gets my back up.

"Honey, take out the garbage."

"What? How dare you make demands like that on me and my valuable time! Can't you see that football is on?"

Then there are clients like Andy, who would regularly come

to my office saying things like, "John, Mandy is making me go to McDonald's to eat lunch!"

"What did she say?"

"She asked me if I wanted to go to McDonald's for lunch."

"What do you think you should do?"

"I want to go to McDonald's for lunch."

"Sounds like a reasonable compromise to me, Andy."

Every request was an unreasonable demand as far as Andy was concerned.

David showed up one morning with a brand new lunch box. He was obviously very proud of his new lunch box. He was showing everybody his new lunch box. The day he showed up with that brand new lunch box happened to be a day when he was scheduled (yes, he had asked to be scheduled) to be in a nutrition activity where clients plan and fix their lunch. For some unfathomable reason, staff told him to put away his brand new lunch box in order to prepare for lunch.

They didn't just tell him once… they repeated it until he finally reached the assaultive stage and kicked the heck out of a staff person. That's an unnecessary demand. It wouldn't have hurt a darned thing if he had taken his new lunch box into the kitchen.

Demanding compliance from a client at any time is a bad behavior that needs to be changed (little joke there…). Give clients a chance to make a good choice and reward (reinforce) them for making the good choice. Also, if you are telling a client to do something or go somewhere, tell them why. They are not children to be ordered about. Why is it important for them to come to the bus stop with you right now? "Because the bus is coming and we might miss it." Just a directive of "Come on!" doesn't let them know why and what is going on.

Change the time and location of activities. Does Jean really need to eat lunch right at 12:00? Would 11:45 or 12:15 work just as well? Or does Jean have a routine where she *does* need to eat right at 12:00? Does Tim really need to use the computer in a busy crowded, noisy room? Is there a computer anywhere else that he could use where he isn't subjected to so many distractions?

Rearrange the environment. Consider that people with claustrophobia may not be able to sit in the middle of a crowded room at a table with a bunch of people. They may need to sit at a small table next to a window. A person who was sexually abused may not be able to sit near a restroom if their abuse happened in a restroom.

I presume that you are familiar with the concept of a "behavioral chain?" Severe behavioral problems are often part of a behavioral chain that progresses from less to more severe. Tapping fingers on a table might lead to whining, which might lead to demanding, which might lead to hitting, etc. There are ways to interrupt a behavioral chain:

Proximity control – we might observe that a person is less likely to display serious behaviors when another person is in close proximity. Moving in closer to a person may interrupt the behavioral chain. Moving *away* may also be the appropriate thing to do. Know the person you are dealing with! Consider that a woman who has been sexually abused by a man might not like a male staff rushing in to put his arms around her to "comfort her."

Inject humor – Carefully! Again, know the person you are dealing with. Many of our clients have been teased about their disability all their life and they don't get humor.

Speaking of humor, Eric came to the door where a co-worker and I were meeting one morning. He announced that he was going to get married. We knew him and knew he could take some teasing, so we asked who would marry him. He named a female client. We started in on him, "She wouldn't marry you, Eric, you're too tall." He took it for a while, and we recognized that it was time to back off. Suddenly he slammed his foot on the floor and said, "OK, you guys, I can either get married or I can live my own life!" We almost bit off our tongues to keep from laughing out loud at him. Boy, did he get that one right!

Watch out for biting sarcasm, too. "Oh, yeah, you learned *that* skill real good, didn't you, Sparky!"

Instructional control – something as simple as instructions may interrupt the behavioral chain. Tell the client what you expect to happen. "Trish, please stop that," may well result with Trish stopping whatever it is. "Remember, when we get into the store, let's not put anything into our backpacks unless we have paid for it and have a receipt." "Bob, please get up off the floor and tell me what is wrong."

When doing this, be careful how you phrase your instructions. Avoid "you" statements. "You need to stop that!" "You need to put that back!" "You need to get up off the floor!" An aggressive statement from you might bring an aggressive response from the client. "I need you to stop that so I can talk to you." "I need you to stop hitting me. My nose is beginning to swell." These are called "assertive" statements. "It sure would be helpful if you would put that chair down so someone could sit in it."

Yes, you in the back with your hand up? What? Does this always work? No. Please keep in mind that I am talking about interim management principles here. This is your "in the meantime" plan.

How about facilitated relaxation? Acknowledge that the person is upset and instruct them to calm down. "I'm sorry you are upset. It's a bummer that we aren't going to a coffee shop first, but it's what the group as a whole decided on. Take a big deep breath with me and let's take a look at the list we made this morning. Oooohmmmmmm…"

Stimulus change – introduce something new or make slight changes in the existing activity. "This seems a bit overwhelming right now. How about we go do (this) for a few minutes?"

Just remember that these methods will most likely only

produce temporary breaks in the behavioral chain. Repeated use of the same method will quickly lose its effectiveness.

I did it again, didn't I? I'm supposed to be telling you what I mean by social and behavioral skills training. Sometimes I get sidetracked.

Chapter 5 – Jobs

Social and behavioral skills training: in order to live as independently as possible there are certain skills that a person needs. If a client wants a job, for example... and excuse me, but why is there such an all out push to make sure all people with a developmental disability have a job? I have heard some absolutely incredible stories about people with disabilities getting "jobs."

I heard about a woman who likes to ride in cars and listen to music, so someone "got her a job" as the owner of an airporter business. Someone bought her a van and hired someone to drive her and paying customers from the airport to hotels. The woman with the disability rides along and puts on her favorite music CD's for everyone to listen to. That's having a job? Please!

I had someone actually tell me about someone he heard about who got a job – he wasn't sure doing what – and the man was in a coma! Well, butter my butt and call me a biscuit. I keep saying, "You come and ask a couple of our clients what job they want and when they tell you, I will do my darndest to get them that job."

How about the person who got a "job" delivering newspapers? She is in a motorized wheelchair and her job is to follow along with a person on a bike who carries the papers. When they get to a house, the woman in the wheelchair announces whether or not it is a house that gets a paper, then the person with the papers gets off their bike and delivers the paper. Yet, the woman in the wheelchair is the one with a "job." Excuse, me, but that's one task of a job. It's great that she has learned that one task, but that isn't "having a job." That's being in a training program.

I was in a meeting once regarding a man in our program who is profoundly (yeah, it's a label, get over it) mentally retarded. The man brings "toys" from home to play with. His "toys" are things like a metal paint roller. Sometime during the day these "toys" would become missiles as the person tried to communicate something to us behaviorally since he is nonverbal. An expert who was at the meeting suggested that we get him a job in a hardware store since he likes paint rollers... and he was serious!

Like I said; incredible: not credible; seeming too unusual to be possible.

Is your job really all that makes you the person that you are? People with disabilities can't be a "whole person" unless they have a job?

If you listen to some people, sheltered workshops are the scourge of the earth. Day programs like ours that offer any form of vocational training are the other scourge of the earth. We're "scourges."

I've never worked for a program that taught "pre-vocational" skills. I'm not sure what that is. It gets you ready for a "pre-job?" That's like saying, "I'm fixin' to get ready to get a job." I have a suspicion it's just what someone calls their vocational training program. It doesn't bother me a bit that they call their program something different than what we call ours. I know that "Supported Employment" is on the outs with the PC crowd. "Customized Employment" is the new phrase. That enables people to find "jobs" like playing music in a van, for people with developmental disabilities. And the rationalization is that people need to experience community based jobs versus sheltered workshop jobs in order to make an informed decision about where they want to work. And what about clients who have experienced both work settings and still choose a sheltered workshop?

We teach vocational skills to our clients who decide that they are ready to learn some work skills. Real work skills. They are basic skills to be sure, but we work with adults, some of whom grew up in state mental institutions, who never had the opportunity, or even the perception of their right, to learn these basic skills. No one is going to go get a job in the community shredding paper with the skills we teach them in our program. That's not the expectation. And that's why sometimes we pay a commensurate wage instead of minimum wage to our trainees while they learn basic vocational skills. We offer the opportunity to learn skills like:

Standards of Work Performance:

Punctuality and Attendance
Dress and Hygiene
Reaction to Supervisor
Getting On With Other Workers
Concentration
Work Area
Behavior Regulation
Communication
Memory Performance

Vocations:

What Kind Of Job Do I Want?
What Kinds Of Jobs Are There?
Required Job Skills

Job Search:

Where Do I Look For A Job?
How Do I Contact An Employer?
Job Applications
Your Resume
The Job Interview

I Got The Job, Now What?:

Work Ethics
Job Rules
Job Productivity
Job Quality
ADA

These are all segments in our SNAP Curriculum, too. Coincidence? I wonder... No one is born with all of these skills. They are learned.

Is there anyone out there who truly believes it is up to employers in your city/town to teach these skills to their employees? If you are a manager and you do any hiring for your program, are you looking for people with no qualifications of any kind so you can spend the time to teach them? How many of you have a minimum requirement of a high school degree (or equivalent) for your hiring practices? How many of you are hiring adults with profound or even severe mental retardation to be your staff people? Why not? I'm sure that you could then teach them to handle their assaultive behavior while you pay them a full paycheck with benefits like your other employees get... and be responsible for completing their job assignments.

Am I being ridiculous? Am I being ridiculous?

Could it be that one reason it is difficult to place some adults with developmental disabilities in community employment is because sometimes we are trying to send them people who are really unprepared to work... unprepared to hold a job once it is secured? Are we in such a hurry to feel good about ourselves?

I am a firm believer that every person who wants a job deserves the chance to have one. That includes homeless people, seniors, you, me, and people with developmental disabilities. But I also believe we are doing a real disservice when we attempt to place people without the basic skills necessary to hold a job. It's one thing to make reasonable accommodations for a person to do a job. It's another thing to expect an employer to do our job for us.

I say again, you come and talk to a couple of our clients and when they clearly indicate their choice of a job to you, I promise that I will make every attempt possible to help them get that job. But until they have had the opportunity to be exposed to some basic job skills training, and to visit a variety of job sites so that they have the chance to make an informed decision, leave us alone!

Are there agencies out there that don't have a clue? I have no doubt. Does that make the whole system corrupt? No. How about providing some standards of training for agencies that need help? How about figuring out that every small town in America doesn't have a lot of job openings? How about asking the clients if they want a job in a sheltered workshop or "in the community"? If you are going to talk about person centered planning and self determination, then it might be time to start listening to the people you are "advocating" for.

OK, I really got up on my soapbox that time, didn't I? Well, no apologies.

Chapter 6 – Community Based

One more thing… one of the "new concepts" is about getting rid of programs like ours that provide training in group settings in and out of our facility. Currently, our basic program is a 1:3 ratio. No, no, you have to be fully community based and 1:1 or 1:2 at worst! "Site-less programs" or "programs without walls" are the big new thing. All clients, including those who are medically fragile, or lack the physical stamina or desire, must spend their entire day "out in the community." Of course, then we have Service Coordinators from our funding source who won't refer clients to our program because we "spend too much of our time in the community."

There's some real person centered planning for you. Can you say, "Catch-22"?

Remember the joke I told about tomatoes being green little hard things? We live in a small town where it rains a lot in the winter and it rains hard. But that doesn't matter. If we aren't "in the community", we are apparently doing our clients a disservice. It doesn't matter if your program has a lot of seniors who really don't want to go out into the community for 5 or 6 hours per day; no community all day, then you are a bad program. There aren't a lot of stores, museums, etc. in our rural area to visit, but no matter. If we aren't in the community, shame on us. Could the seniors go to the community senior center where other community seniors go? Possibly. We believe that it depends on a person's behavior issues, medical needs, personal choice... and no, I am not saying that this is carte blanch for programs to never provide training opportunities in the community because a client has a "behavioral problem." All clients regardless of behavioral issues have the right to participate in the community. All day every day might not always be the best for them, though.

Most of our clients bring a sack lunch to program. There aren't a lot of places to eat a sack lunch in our community... especially when it's pouring rain. But no matter, if we aren't in the community, then we aren't complying with current progressive thinking. Let your clients eat their sack lunch in McDonald's and don't worry about what other community members think. It isn't about them, it's about being community based. Besides, it's nice for the community to see those "poor retarded kids" out having lunch on "field trips" like that. It attracts a lot of attention. Aaargh! I really don't think that's the image we're trying for.

Those kinds of perceptions are much less likely to occur if we are eating a Big Mac in McDonald's like everybody else, instead of eating a sack lunch.

Yes, you with your hand up in the back? What? Why doesn't everybody just get a Big Mac for lunch? Because we can't afford to pay our staff enough to eat out every day. What? Oh, you mean the clients? Yeah, well...

And somehow, programs like ours get the blame for a broken system?

Look, I know there isn't a lot of money floating around, and people with developmental disabilities aren't a big voting block, but until we can pay even close to a living wage (whatever that is for sure) for providing quality services, we are going to keep suffering huge staff turnover, and that affects the quality of programming. I heard a speaker from Canada once who said, "I don't know how it is in the U.S., but in Canada, staff turnover is on Thursdays." I know how he feels. I spend a lot of my time hiring and orienting new staff people. Our current facility has been open for more than 5 years. My secretary and I are the only ones here who were here when we opened.

It's been said that to most clients, a stranger is just a staff person they haven't met yet. "Mary, you don't know Barney, but he is your new staff person. Do everything he tells you tonight…"

If you want to stress over labels, how the label of "entry level job." That's what our work is considered… entry level. Anybody can do this. "Whut. You go into town with some people and have a coke at McDonald's. Big deal." Yeah… except for needing the ability to perform behavioral assessments in order to determine the communicative intent of a behavior… and then discover a behavior that replaces the dysfunctional one… and figure out how to teach that new behavior… and ensure the safety of people with minimal street safety skills while in the community… and deal with assaultive behaviors and mental health issues and medical issues. Yeah, anybody can do this job. Why don't you come on down and put in an application?

And again, I say that people like me can sit and complain or we can do what we can do. I strive to provide the best training I can for my staff so that I don't add to their stress by sending them out to do a job unprepared. I give them the best tools and information I can and I give them the opportunity to do their jobs. And with all that, some of them still can't feed and clothe their families on minimum wage. I don't get it.

Chapter 7 – Ethical Issues

I worked with a woman once who decided that she "loved me." We had a number of talks about the fact that I am married, and while I could be her friend, I was a staff person and she and I weren't going to have a relationship. She would agree for a day or so, then she was back to "loving me." It got to be kind of a problem because she would refuse to go out in any training activities unless she could go with me.

Well, one day in her ISP meeting, at the end of the meeting I asked her if she wanted to say anything else about her program. She said, "Yes." Then she looked directly at me and said, "I love you." We all smiled and I said, "I think you mean you like me."

She didn't bat an eye. In a throaty voice she just said, "Yeah. I like you… a-lahhhhhht."

One of my favorite clients was Jerry. Jerry is blind, but he always knew it was me offering an arm to help him maneuver about… except that he often didn't want to go the direction I wanted us to go… even if we were trying to walk out through a door. He would exclaim, "No, not that way!" and pull away from me. I would patiently explain that I was pointing him towards the door, but he would insist, "No, not that way."

I would finally give up and let him go. He would turn and invariably crash into a wall. I would then ask, "Ready?" At which time he would cheerfully take my arm and exit the room with me, stroking the hair on my arm and saying, "Nice John."

Those are a couple of my favorite stories... and there's a point to telling them here. Sometimes there are things that happen during the day with clients that you just have to share with someone. Be careful where you share stories and with whom. Remember confidentiality. There is no need to identify people in your program to the community.

We don't wear t-shirts with our agency name or wear name tags. We don't tell people what we are doing as we go along during the day. We are just some folks out in the community like everyone else today. We don't walk along like a "row of ducks" with staff up front and clients behind. It's important to be aware of these things when you are engaged in training activities in the community.

And for gosh sakes, please don't ever make your adult clients hold hands with other clients as you go on your merry way throughout the community. I had a staff do that once. He made a client hold the hand of a more severely disabled peer while they were in the community... "for safety." I found out about it when the client quit the program because, as he said, "I don't want to have to hold the hand of a retarded person while we are out." That staff person didn't last long in our program. He couldn't get over the fact that the adults in our program were not "just like children" as he had been told his whole life. That's OK. This line of work is not for everyone.

Possibly the most important concern surrounding social and behavioral skills training is/are ethical issues. I hope it comes as a surprise to no one to hear that people with developmental disabilities have the same rights as you and me. They enjoy all the usual rights; life, liberty and the pursuit of happiness. In my state we have a law that assures rights for people with developmental disabilities. It's called the Lanterman Act. It was written in the 1960's and it promises services and supports to people with developmental disabilities and their families (unfortunately, it doesn't promise adequate funding to provide those services and supports).

Included in those client's rights is the right to make choices about your own life and to get the services and supports you need to be a member of your community. I assume everyone is familiar with "informed consent"? Clients should be able to ask questions and receive reasonable answers about their programs. They have a right to attend meetings (such as an ISP) whether we consider them able to participate fully or not. It's *their* meeting about them. They should be able to be there and participate to the extent that they can or want to. They should be able to invite whomever they want to their meeting as part of their support team. I know a woman who invites one of her peers to every meeting.

Informed consent means that the person has been exposed to a variety of options and they make a choice, expressing in some way that they understand. Just you explaining - no matter in how much detail - what is going on doesn't count as informed consent. What do you see (hmmm... a behavior) that tells you they understand and agree? This means that you have to know the person well enough to know their signs of acknowledgement... whether they are verbal or not. Lots of clients agree with anything a staff person says because they have been taught to comply all their life. Remember how I talked about the fact that we are not after compliance? We want clients to make assertive, informed decisions. Is this always going to happen? No. That's when a person's support team may have to make some decisions for them, hopefully in the client's best interest and not just what is easiest for the team members or what sounds good on paper.

Sometimes, especially in rural areas, there aren't a lot of choices about available services. This doesn't necessarily mean that the system is broken and we need new labels and to change everything. Sometimes it just means that it is a rural area without a lot of choices available. People still have the right to make informed consent choices from what is available.

"Yeah, well, people with developmental disabilities don't need 'services'. They need to be able to live their lives like the rest of us"... I have heard someone say.

Actually, I use a number of community services. Life is full of services. I use a service that hauls away my garbage. I don't have a choice about services for garbage because there is only one garbage company, and I don't always like the service I get, but that's life. Same with my TV cable company. Sometimes we just have to use what is available and make the best of it. It isn't necessarily the case manager's "fault" that they placed a client in a day program. Maybe it is what was available and we have to go with it until more services are available... or until the client is ready to try another service... making their own informed decision. I suppose there is some chance that the client chose that day program after visiting. It could happen.

And please don't say that a bad garbage company doesn't hurt me, but a bad service program can hurt a client. If a program is that bad, someone should be shutting down that particular program and horsewhipping (or some other Type I or Type II punishment) the people who run it. It doesn't mean that all day programs are faulty. Or better yet, maybe somebody could go in and provide some training to the staff to make them a better agency.

Back to rights. I often have to remind my staff that while clients have the same rights as you and I, they don't have any extra ones. While a client has the "right" to throw a big tantrum while in line at the bank, and fall to the floor yelling and screaming, the bank also has the "right" to toss them out. People with developmental disabilities don't have the right to "get away with inappropriate behaviors" just because they have a disability. And just because they have the option to tantrum, it doesn't make it socially appropriate. I had a store manager call me and apologize because he had just asked a client and her staff to leave his business because she (the client) was vocalizing at the top of her lungs.

I asked him what he would do if anyone else came into his store and started yelling. He said he would ask them to leave. I said, "Then it sounds like you did the right thing this time, too." The store owner's actions were a natural consequence of yelling in a store. He was surprised, because he has been told all his life that people with disabilities are just like children...

Whose fault is it that the store owner views people with disabilities this way? Is it our fault as a day program? Is it the fault of the people who complain and want to have "better services" (although apparently we shouldn't label them "services"...) instead of spending their time providing community education?

Part of the reason that we very often provide skills training in the community is to educate the community-at-large. The more people see us and interact with us, the more acceptance there will be. We have seen it already. When we first opened our center, people in coffee shops eyed us warily when we came in. They weren't sure how to view us... with fear that our clients might "do something", or with pride in our staff for doing such wonderful things with these "kids".

Now when we go in a coffee shop, people are more likely to say, "Hey, Robert, Charlene, how ya doin'?" And they aren't talking to staff.

Not long ago one of my support staff was in a local store observing one of our groups (we do monthly quality checks, I'm sure you probably do, too). When the group left, the clerks began to talk, not realizing that my staff person was actually with the group. They were asking each other if they had "handled" the group OK. My staff introduced herself and assured them that they had acted just fine. They were relieved, since they didn't know exactly how to talk to those "kids". Linda took the time to let them know that it is OK for them to talk to these adults as adults.

Staff at a local natural history museum recently asked me to come talk to them about adults with developmental disabilities. One of their questions was, "Should we give them coloring books like we do for all the kids?" I assured them that if they gave all people – adults as well as children – a coloring book, then absolutely yes, they should give these adults one too. Otherwise... not so much.

How often have you been out with clients and a store clerk turns to you and asks what the adult standing right in front of them would like? Oy! We usually smile and pretend like we just happened to be standing there and say, "I don't know. Why don't you ask him?" I think it's fair to say that most of our clients hate being treated like they aren't even there. It's bad enough when strangers do it to them... can you imagine how it must feel when a trusted person like a staff person slips up and does it?

I often wish, and have suggested, that our funding source (in California we have Regional Centers) would provide some community education, maybe starting with the chamber of commerce or someplace like that, instead of ignoring the issue or hoping that we in the day programs will find time to do it. Our society has come a long way, but there's still a long way to go. All we can do is what each of us can do.

We take client confidentiality very seriously at our facility. When a behavioral incident does occur in the community, there are some very specific things we can't and shouldn't say: "Sorry. This is Barbara and she's mentally retarded. I'm her staff and I'm trying to teach her not to act this way, but she's really slow about getting it."

That's a staff person that I'm going to fire because *they* are so slow about "getting it." But, he says proudly, *my* staff would never do such a stupid thing. We all carry business cards and we might say something like, "Sorry, she is trying to tell me something and I'll get it in a minute." If the person gets insistent, we give them a card and tell them to call and talk to the director. It's also OK to tell people that you can't give out confidential information if you need to.

Since we live in a small town, most people are pretty good about letting us work with public behavioral issues. We have a man in our program who has an issue with clowns. I don't mean silly staff people, I mean clowns. He and a couple of his peers and a staff person went into McDonald's one day for a soda. The store manager had just put up a life size plastic sign in the shape of Ronald McDonald. Fred attacked it. I mean, down on the floor, wrestling with Ronald McDonald.

Everyone in the restaurant was staring at the staff person who was talking to Fred about what was going on. The manager came out and asked what he was going to do. The staff person said, "I'm not going to wrestle with him. I recommend you don't either. Here's one of my business cards. If you need to call the police, call the police." They waited a minute until Fred began to gain the upper hand and finally broke the head off of Ronald, got up and got into line for his soda. The manager let them all stay and have their soda.

Was that rewarding Fred for his behavior by letting him have a soda? Yes. Yes it was. But sometimes you have to pick and choose your fights. If you know anything about assaultive behaviors at all, you know that recovery is not the time to get into consequences. Let the person recover, then direct them back into their plan.

The point here is that staff didn't violate any confidentiality rules even though it was a reasonably serious incident in a very public place, and the store manager had every right to call the police if he wanted to. Sometimes, the police are a natural consequence of behaviors.

When we are sitting on a public transit bus and someone gestures towards one of our clients and asks, "What do they have?" meaning what's *wrong* with them... we say, "She has a lovely smile, don't you think so?"

We had a client... I just noticed how many times I'm saying, "We *had* a client in our program..."That's because some of our clients actually do move on to other programs and systems of support. Not everybody is "stuck" in our day program for the rest of their life.

Anyway, we had a client named Chris who has cerebral palsy and he sort of "lumbers about" when he walks. His speech is somewhat difficult to understand, too. Chris loves people and he loves to come up and say hi to them. Unfortunately, his way of doing that is almost always to suddenly appear right in their face from behind and shout, "Your name?!" Scares the heck out of people.

I worked with him about a way that might be more appropriate, such as approaching them from the front, making some eye contact to see if they want to be approached, then using an indoor voice to ask, "Your name?" He got pretty good at it, but there were always the people who, when he forgot and surprised them, and once they got over their initial fright, would be "helpful" and say, "That's all right. My name is..."

I couldn't – and wouldn't – explain that "This is Chris and I'm working with him not to scare people like that." I would say, "Chris, may I see you for a minute?" His lip would come out and tremble. We would move to the side and I would say, "You're not in trouble, but remember how we talked...?"

The person was trying to be helpful, but who is Chris going to believe – me and my story about approaching people, or the person he just scared who said it was OK? All I could do was keep reminding Chris about social manners.

Oh, another story about Chris... Chris had a job delivering our local shopper paper through our program. I walked his route with him, helping him remember the whole route. One day, he walked up to a house to leave the paper in its bag on the door knob. I waited for him at the curb.

Sure enough, just as he got to the door, the guy who lives there happened to come out the door. That was too much of a temptation for Chris. "Your name?!" he shouted.

He no more than got the words out when a dog came rushing out the door, growling, and jumped up and grabbed Chris by the arm.

The guy just about had a heart attack. *I* just about had a heart attack. I rushed up and the guy pulled the dog away. Chris stood there calmly, then looked at the guy and shouted, "Your dog's name?!" The dog had only gotten his sleeve. Not a mark on Chris.

People wanting to "help" are often a nuisance. "Here, let me buy her that toy so she will quiet down." "Here, let me buy him that bag of chips, package of hot dogs and case of soda." We usually smile and remind the client that maybe it would be better to wait until s/he has enough money to make his/her own purchases. There is no need to direct an explanation to the community member. They usually get what is going on.

Always be aware of public perception while in the community. I have received phone calls from concerned community members who just saw one of my staff "wrestle a client to the ground." They missed the part about the speeding truck that the client was standing in front of.

We had a woman in program who was mostly non-verbal. I say "mostly" because she did know the word "no." She knew it very well. If fact, she would yell that word at the top of her lungs sometimes. Didn't matter if she was in a good mood or not. She just liked the word; no. Due to some safety and behavioral concerns, she had a 1:1 Tutor. One of her male Tutors once told me to expect a call someday saying he had been arrested. It seems there was more than once that he was assisting her in the restroom in the community while she was happily yelling "no" at the top of her lungs.

That's why we provide signs that say – an attendant of the opposite sex may be in this restroom – for staff to carry, as well as their business cards. It is in our job descriptions that we may have to assist a person with personal hygiene. It is never in the client's plan for them to have to be in a restroom stall with you while you go to the bathroom. Plan your day well!

And remember, you as a staff person are modeling behavior for the public as well as your clients. If you talk to clients as though they are children, so will the general public. If you yell across a crowded restaurant, "Susie, we're getting ready to go, so go to the bathroom!" you are displaying that Susie is a child who needs to be "taken care of". Maybe Susie doesn't need to go to the restroom.

Stealing is an issue we deal with on a regular basis. Again, clients have rights. If a client steals something, it is not your place to snatch it out of their hand and put it back to avoid any embarrassment. You can certainly counsel the client about stealing and identify possible consequences (without making it a threat), and offer them a way out. "Would you like to put that back until you have enough money to buy it or would you like me to put it back for you?"

Rob took a candy bar from the shelf in a video store one day. I saw him do it, so I casually asked him if he had enough money to pay for it. No, he didn't. "Would you like to put it back or would you like me to put it back for you?" Neither one. "Well, you know, Rob, if you take it and don't pay for it, that's called stealing and that's against the law. I would have to tell the store clerk and he might call the police and I can't protect you from that." Nothing doing.

So I quietly told the clerk. The clerk, looking at Rob, who obviously has Down syndrome, announced in a loud voice, "That's OK, he can have it."

"Cool," I said. "Hey everybody, have a candy bar, they're free!"

The clerk almost wet himself. "Wait! Wait!"

"I thought you said he could have the candy bar without paying for it?"

By then, Rob realized I was serious and he was right by my side handing the candy bar back. I didn't have to break any confidentiality laws, I didn't embarrass Rob by accusing him of "being a thief" in front of people, and the clerk learned a lesson. It was a good day.

Again, calling the police for theft is a natural consequence for stealing.

Clients have rights regarding their personal property, too. Just because they are in your program doesn't give you the right to go through their personal stuff (except for contraband). We provide lockers to staff and clients if they want one. I wouldn't dream of going through any staff person's personal locker. Why would I think it was OK to rummage through a client's locker? Or go through their backpack or lunchbox?

If a staff needs to get in a client's backpack to assist a client in making a purchase because the client can't go through their own backpack and get their money out, for example, I had better hear staff ask permission (even if it is a severely disabled non-verbal person – boy, there's a bunch of labels!) to get their money out for them.

Wheelchairs – I tell my staff to just consider a person's wheelchair as an extension of their body. You don't generally lean on a person when you are talking to them… don't lean on a person's wheelchair. Don't use a person's wheelchair to carry your coat and backpack during the day. Do your friends carry your stuff for you all the time? Yeah, maybe when you were a cheerleader in high school.

Don't ever move a person in their wheelchair without asking them first. I have seen too many times when a staff person moved someone so that they or another person could "squeeze past." Would you like it if someone just shoved you aside so that they could walk past you? It is always a good idea to talk to the client about why they should pay attention to where they have stopped their wheelchair so that they aren't blocking an aisle, but don't just shove them aside.

Stranger awareness is probably the hardest thing we try to teach. Like I said before, to many clients, a stranger is just a staff person they haven't met yet. Clients have a right to talk to anyone they want to. The best we can do is to try to get clients to understand about personal information versus private information, and which would you be willing to share with someone you don't know?

Personal information may include things like the name of the town you live in. Private information might be your actual address. Personal information might include the fact that you work at McDonald's. Private information might be how much you make per hour and what days you get paid.

You might share casual personal information with someone who sits next to you on the bus and they ask if you live here. You might say, "Yes, I live in (name of your town)." But you wouldn't give them your address and telephone number.

Private information is shared with family, close friends and professionals such as a doctor or your direct care staff. If your doctor asks how you feel, you would give him all the details you can. If a store clerk asks how you feel, you wouldn't tell them about your constipation and how you haven't gone to the bathroom for three days…

Chapter 8 – Assaultive Behaviors

Can we talk about assaultive behaviors for a minute? I'm no expert, but let me share a couple of things I do know. Assaultive behaviors are still behaviors. They are something you can see and measure. They are a form of communication. They are a way the client is attempting to get a need met. Assaultive behavior is part of that behavioral chain I talked about in chapter 4.

Assaultive behaviors generally go though a recognizable set of stages:

The Trigger – What started this? Triggers may or may not be observable. One client hitting another may be a trigger. A flashback to a previous event may be a trigger.

Escalation – Tapping fingers insistently moves to verbal whining, which leads to verbal demands, which leads to pulling at your sleeve which leads to…

The Assault – Biting, kicking, hitting, spitting, etc.

Recovery – The client seems to recognize what they have just done and they take a step back. Let them have a moment without getting on their case.

Depression – The client may cry and need to be left alone at this point. Don't hand out consequences now either. This is the time to direct them back into their activity/plan.

The behavior management strategies I talked about earlier

were ways to interrupt the behavioral chain up to the point of assault.

Two really good ways to possibly break a behavioral chain are:

- Active Listening – trying to understand what the person is feeling, making a statement of your guess, and waiting for them to confirm or deny. Staff makes a "Here's what I heard you say," statement;

    Client: "I can't do this!" (as they bang their fist on the table).

    Staff: "What I am hearing you say is that you feel frustrated because you can't fold that card correctly."

    Client: "Yeah"… or the client response may be, "No, I don't want to fold cards right now. I want to go check my e-mail."

    Making a statement like; "Grow up! You can do it. Just try harder," puts you well on the way to being assaulted.

- Talk to Adults as an Adult – one of the easiest ways to get a client to lose respect for you is to talk to them as if they were a child. Never make the mistake of believing that because a person acts out behaviors at a 5 year old's developmental level, that the person *is* 5 years old (where have I heard that before?). That's why it's called a "developmental disability". They probably haven't had the chance to develop a 50 year old's socially appropriate way of handling situations.

    I personally am a fan of Piaget's definitions of developmental levels:

1. Sensorimotor (0 to 4 years) Explores things that can be seen, felt, touched; develops motor skills.

2. Preoperational (2 to 7 years) Thinks in terms of self; oriented to the present; intuitive rather than logical.

3. Concrete operations (7 to 11 years) Begins to understand numbers, space, and classification and to apply logical operations to concrete problems; thinking is bound to the concrete.

4. Formal operations (11 to 15 years) Able to think abstractly, hypothesize, generalize, reason and form different standpoints, and to develop ideals.

Consider that preschool age kids often have difficulty controlling explosive outbursts and are easily provoked by hearing the word "no," or by sharing issues.

Elementary school age kids may have issues around friendship or possessions.

Early adolescents often turn their attention from peers to figures of authority and, lacking judgment, may pick a fight with someone who can beat the heck out of them.

Late adolescents may fight over male-female relationships and be subject to intense peer pressure.

What developmental level are your clients and how does that impact the way they learn new things and handle situations that are out of their routine? What does it mean to "act like a 5 year old?" And how do you handle it when an adult does act that way?

Joe is a guy who will test you. He will make a statement such as, "Today is Tuesday," and then he waits to see what you say. If you speak to him like he is a child, "No, Joe, today is Wednesday... remember, Monday, Tuesday, Wednesday, Thursday..." he will walk away assured that you are an idiot and he won't place much trust in you.

He is much more reassured if you say something like, "What is this... a test? I think you know what day today is."

And please, if you cannot understand the speech of a person with cerebral palsy, never smile and say," Uh, huh, that's nice," and turn away. Linda is a woman with cerebral palsy who assured me that giving up on her speech was one of the most frustrating things in her life. She would rather you spend a half hour saying, "I'm sorry, can you say that again? I didn't quite get it," than to treat her like a child and walk away. She wanted to beat people with a stick who did that to her.

Can you possibly imagine walking away while the person is trying to tell you that their mother just passed away? "Oh, that's nice... good for you!" And a big "thumbs up".

You may read other places (or you can read it here) about "Operant" and "Respondent" behaviors (yeah, I know some of them college words). Operant behaviors are voluntary and external – you are doing unto others by choice. This includes behaviors motivated by manipulation and intimidation, for example. Keep in mind that these behaviors may be done without the client sitting down and giving careful consideration as to whether the behaviors may work on you or not and then making the decision to give it a try. They may be what the person has learned that works for them during their life, and it has become an automatic response because it works.

Respondent behaviors are involuntary and internal – you can't help feeling the way you do in response to a stimulus. Examples may include behaviors motivated by fear and frustration. It doesn't matter if we think the fear is real or not. It only has to matter to the client and it may be as simple (to us) as being afraid that they don't have enough stuff in their lunch today, and they may starve.

Blinking (something's in my eye) is respondent. Winking (hey, baby!) is operant. Getting goose pimples when you are cold is respondent behavior. You don't consciously get goose pimples. "Wow, its cold, I better get some goose pimples!" Putting on your jacket to warm up is operant behavior.

Respondent behaviors caused by fear (they can't help feeling afraid) could lead to assaultive behavior. Operant behaviors stemming from intimidation (they are attempting to control the environment with threats) could also lead to assaultive behavior.

When dealing with assaultive behaviors, you might want to determine whether the behavior is operant or respondent to know how to respond to it.

See, knowing something about these kinds of concepts could help make your job easier. Training has to start somewhere and if it starts here and now, fine. Ah, ha! There *is* a point to all of this. I know I can ramble sometimes and it seems like I don't know where I'm going, but...

OK, the point...

The more programs that know what they are doing, the more the people dedicated to scrapping the system and starting over can find something else to do. It isn't the labels that make a program ineffective – it's a lack of training.

Chapter 9 – Reasons for Behavior

We know the definition of a behavior and we know that behaviors are ways we all get our needs met. But what are some causes of behaviors? Remember that many of our adult clients have been trained their whole life to comply with whatever they are told. We are not after compliance. At our day program, we are trying to teach people to be assertive, to advocate for themselves, and to make their own independent choices whenever possible.

There are many reasons for behaviors. One way or another, the behavior is done to get a need met, but what might cause the need? The reasons are not always obvious to us. Behaviors may seem to be "out of the blue", but there is always a reason.

Behaviors may occur in response to any number of physical, emotional, environmental or other kinds of conditions:

Medical conditions – has a good medical check been done on a client displaying new or recurring negative behaviors? Often a client cannot tell a doctor that, "I have a sharp pain right here when I take a deep breath." Verbal or not, they may sit quietly and stare at the doctor, or they may sit and bang on the examining table… or on the doctor. Therefore, their level of care can be less than what is necessary.

This is assuming that someone takes the client to the doctor in the first place and doesn't wait to see what happens because there isn't a staff person available right now.

Whenever you see a new behavior – either positive or negative – suspect a change in medication. Every medication has side effects. When a client can't stay awake during the day, it may not be that you are an incredibly boring person. It could be a medicine side effect. Check it out. Also check out to see if you *are* an incredibly boring person and they don't even want to be where they are right now, but check medicines, too.

Cognitive awareness – do we understand their cognitive level? How do *they* learn things? Consider that people with developmental disabilities often have problems with abstractions. We can tell them what we want, but maybe they just can't picture what we are saying. Remember, it has been said that a camel is a horse put together by a committee. Each person is picturing something different from a spoken description.

If you ask Paul if he would take a cookie from a stranger, he will look at you like you are a nut and say," No way!" However, if you take Paul out into the community and a stranger approaches with a bag of cookies, Paul is all over them like white in a snowstorm. Why? You do constant stranger awareness training… why doesn't he get it? Talking about what a stranger is, is an abstraction… you are hoping that Paul will "make the connection" from your clever descriptions and pictures. We go into the community and when we see a disheveled, stinky person drinking from a paper bag on the sidewalk, we might say, "See that person there? That person is a stranger to me and I wouldn't take any kind of food from him/her." You have to start somewhere.

Psychiatric conditions – the developmentally disabled population has a higher rate of psychiatric problems, due in part to discrimination - us (as a society, not as individual staff people) telling them their whole life that what they are doing is "wrong," when actually, the behavior may not be wrong, but the time and location sure could be. A person who masturbates on a public transit bus isn't necessarily engaging in a "bad" behavior. The time and location is a bit inappropriate…

Significant life changes – A person moving out of a developmental center to a supported community housing situation is going through a significant life change. A person who has lived with an overprotective parent most of their life, the parent dies, and the person is moved into a group home undergoes a significant life change. Many of us are upset when something interrupts our daily routine – the telephone rings just as our favorite TV show comes on - can you imagine being moved to a new house and no one told you? I know a woman who has had that happen a couple of times in her life. "Nope, sorry, you don't live with Deanne anymore. You live here now."

That woman used to strip off all her clothes and race out the door and across the busy parking lot of a neighboring department store. Once we discovered what had happened in her life, we would ask her if she was worried about her stuff at home when we saw her behavior escalating. We let her call her house and be reassured that she still lived there and all her stuff was OK. She could then make it through the day without stripping and running.

Life space conditions – How much privacy do you get during the day? Can you tell people to go away and leave you alone? Can your clients do that? Even in supported living conditions with no day program? How many of you check on your clients when they have been in the restroom "too long?" Those of us in licensed programs have to check on people as part of our job under 'care and supervision'. Have you ever heard a staff person say (or worse, said it yourself), "OK, but what happened last night with your staff is a 'home' problem. You're at program now, so how about we talk about your schedule for the day?"

Let a client vent if they need to. You don't have to promise to fix anything for them, and venting may release a lot of tension for the client.

Cultural differences – is English the client's primary language? Do they have a religious practice that makes them uncomfortable in some activities (like attending parties or shopping at Victoria's Secret at the mall)? What do you really know about this person's background? What are *your* attitudes about the people you are serving? Are you uncomfortable being around people with disabilities because they embarrass you in public?

Staff training conditions – are you uncomfortable working around people with assaultive behaviors, so you ignore them or are very tentative around them, or refuse to work at all with them? I believe a lot of staff turn-over problems are a result of a lack of training, and then staff are afraid of clients when there is no need to be "afraid' if you know what you are doing. Do you know how to use the prompting hierarchy? Do know the specific reinforcer to use with each Objective of each client you work with? Do you know how to handle assaultive behaviors? Have you read and you understand the person's behavior support plan?

And the main cause… the envelope, please…

Consequences! It has worked before, so I think I'll try it again. Last night when I whined enough, my wife finally fixed dinner. I'm hungry now, so I think I'll whine a little. Yesterday, my staff left me alone when I growled and bared my teeth because I didn't want to work on an art project. I think I'll try that again today to see if I can get out of my work activity. Staff praised me when I asked permission to leave an activity to use the restroom and I liked that. I think I'll ask permission again today if I need to leave an activity.

Caution and beware! Danger! Danger, Will Robinson! A client should never have to ask permission to go to the bathroom! Notifying you that they are leaving an activity so you know what happened to them is one thing – making anyone ask *permission to use the restroom* is never acceptable.

Every client with what we consider a higher needs behavioral issue (aggressive/assaultive behaviors, for example) in our program has a Behavior Support Plan. For us, this is a companion document to their ISP. Some people make them all one plan. Do what works for you and your program.

The Behavior Support Plan gives information about the client – their likes and dislikes, their manner of communication, their social habits (gregarious, shy, etc). It also defines the target behavior very specifically. Why was this document written? Describe the topography of the behavior – what does it look like? - and the cycle of the behavior - when does an incident start? When does an incident end? If Tom hits Jim on the shoulder 10 times quickly in a row, is that 10 incidents or one incident? However you decide to define these things is the correct way for your program. Everyone involved just needs to be on the same page.

One of the most important parts of a Behavior Support Plan is identifying a replacement behavior. What would be a more appropriate way of communicating instead of the current dysfunctional/inappropriate/dangerous behavior? The replacement behavior then becomes an Objective statement in the individual's ISP. It's not enough just to identify the replacement behavior. There has to be a way to teach it to the client.

We also include proactive and reactive interventions. How might we head off an incident? What can we do during an incident?

Behavior issues may be as simple as a client who smokes and thinks whenever and wherever he wants to smoke is appropriate, to a complex assaultive behavior.

Be careful with your plans. Sam is the smoker guy. We can't write a "no smoking" plan for him. He is an adult and has the right to be a smoker. But as long as he chooses to attend our program, there are some basic rules everyone is expected to follow, and we can write a plan to help Sam learn to follow rules about when and where it is appropriate to smoke.

I recently worked on a great plan for a gentleman in our program to reduce his incidents of repeating what other people say. Then I stepped back and read the plan again... OK, someone else pointed it out to me... a plan to reduce his incidents... a plan to stop his "bad"... Oops! My bad.

We are doing some assessments to try to determine why he echoes what he hears. Is it for social attention? "Hey, talk to me instead." Does he have echolalia (the immediate and involuntary repetition of words or phrases spoken by others) and he can't help repeating? Is it to gain some processing time for understanding information? When we find out why the behavior occurs, then we can write a plan for a replacement behavior. How can he gain attention without echoing something he just heard, if that's the function of the behavior?

Remember when we talked about talking to adults like adults? I always know when a staff person inappropriately tells a client to "go to the bathroom because we're almost ready to leave." I know because I can hear Albert clear down the hall at my office, echoing what he just heard staff say. "YEAH, LUCY, GO TO THE BATHROOM BECAUSE WE'RE GETTING READY TO LEAVE!"

Whatever you do, don't be embarrassed to ask for help with behavioral issues. We have had outside consultants come in to help us. Our Resource Specialist (the label for our Behavior guy) and I have been called in to consult with other local agencies. I hate the ones who come in for 30 minutes, observe the client briefly for the first time, and then tell us that "she needs a communication board." Thank you very much.

My favorite consultant was the one who came in, did his

observation, looked at our data and said, "Heck if I know. It looks like you guys have some good data here. Have you tried...?"

And that's probably the key point with behavioral issues. "Have you tried...?" Have you done your assessments? Does the behavior only happen or happens more frequently at certain times? Have you tried moving the time of that activity? Does the behavior only happen or happens more frequently at certain locations? Have you tried moving the activity? Does the behavior only happen or happens more frequently with certain staff? Have you tried using a different staff person?

It doesn't matter what the activity is... eating lunch at home, playing cards with peers at a day program, washing dishes at a restaurant... try different things to see what works.

Why is it important to change some behaviors? Part of our Behavior Support Plan is a risk assessment. The risks may be that someone, including the client, could be injured by the behavior. It may be a risk of social isolation because other people are afraid to be around them. There are lots of risks. Our communities have certain standards that we all live by. If a person has grown up in an environment like a developmental center, and now when they are an adult and we believe that they want an apartment of their own to have an inclusive life, how can we expect them to have the most basic grasp of the community's standards? How can they get a job in the community if they aren't aware of, or haven't had the opportunity to practice, basic behavioral skills such as not screaming at the person working next to them because "He looked at me funny and I don't like it"?

We never deny a person the right to community access because of some previous behavior or what we think might happen later in the day. If a person's behavior at the time of boarding the transit bus is such that it isn't safe for them to board the bus, or is so disruptive that it hangs up the bus schedule, then we can identify possible consequences.

"Wow, Gary, I would sure hate to see you lose this opportunity to go to the zoo with us today because of your behavior right now. How can I help you get control?"

"You calm down this instant or you can't go with us!" is a threat. We don't do threats.

Gary may have to stay at the center or possibly go home for the day if he cannot get control of himself (the technical term is referred to as "getting his act together"), but if he gains control, he goes on with his day and receives positive reinforcement for displaying appropriate behavior.

Make sure you are "catching people when they are good," too. Phillip used to bring a big "boom box" to program with him. He also used to spend most of his day threatening to rip your "f-ing" face off. He is a big guy who could have done that if he really wanted to. Staff would talk to him about how he was feeling and what his needs were and more appropriate ways to communicate, etc. Once in a great while, he would sit quietly at a small table playing his boom box very appropriately so only he could hear it.

You could just see staff relax, and the whisper would echo down the hall... "Phillip is being good... everyone, leave him alone." Actually I would hear Albert down the hall, "YEAH EVERYBODY, PHILLIP IS BEING GOOD, LEAVE HIM ALONE!"

That would last maybe 5 minutes and then Phillip was up threatening to rip someone's "f-ing" face off. I wanted to use a severe form of Type I or Type II punishment on staff when that happened. When he sits down and is not threatening anyone is *the* time to talk to him! Catch him when he is being good. "Hey Phillip, thanks for keeping your radio turned down. I'm helping Susan for a few minutes, but how about when I'm done, you and I play a couple of hands of cards?" Then actually go back and play cards with him!

Yes, you with your hand up in the back. What? Does this work for everyone? No. I'm just telling some stories about how we have handled some situations before. I'm hoping it will get people started thinking about what they do in their programs.

One of the biggest times during our day for behavioral incidents to occur is during transition times. Clients arrive at 8:45, but the first transit bus doesn't come until 9:30. What does everybody do for 45 minutes? Lunch time is an hour, but Debbie eats her lunch in about 5 minutes, then has 55 minutes with nothing to do. You're at the bus stop 5 minutes early and the bus is 5 minutes late. What do you do for 10 minutes? For some people, that's a long time not to be engaged in something or with someone.

Transition times happen to all of us all the time. What do you do when you are stuck in traffic? Has anyone ever had to sit and wait for a meeting to start because someone was late? Ever been to a doctor's office? Most of us just handle it. Many of our clients don't have that "handle it" skill yet.

Chapter 10 – Social Skills Training

What I mean by social skills training:

Pick your label, whether we are teaching people independent living skills or supported living skills, many people in our program just never had the opportunity to learn about our community standards. In our SNAP Curriculum, there is a piece called What Is Appropriate Behavior? That's a phrase we use regularly – "appropriate behavior." Do your clients know what that means? Our people do because we have a curriculum so all staff can review the concept with our clients. Basically, it just means how everybody else acts in our community. Most adult people don't throw tantrums in the middle of the supermarket because they don't have enough money for a soda. Most adults don't tell the transit bus driver what they had for breakfast and ask what the driver's wife is doing right now and what they had for dinner last night.

Most people in our community don't hit another person when they need to use the bathroom or anchor in the bathroom for several hours when they don't want to participate in an activity. Most of us just go use the restroom or ask for help, and most of us would just say, "No thanks, I don't care to do that right now."

One of the hardest things for new staff to get used to is having to think about all the things that we don't think about every day. Yeah, twist your head around that one. When we need to go to K-Mart to get something and we don't have a car, we just get on the bus and go, or ask a friend to take us, "Thanks!" We go in the store, "Oh, excuse me, go ahead, Ma'am," and we pretty much know where things are located in the store so we go get it, or we hunt down a clerk and ask where the widgets are. If they don't have any widgets, we mumble under our breath about "this stupid store," and go on to another store to look for it. We don't stand around and perseverate – how's that for a fancy college word? – or throw ourselves down on the floor, yelling and kicking in frustration.

Yes, you with your hand up in the back? What? Perseverate? It means to engage in the same behavior or thought in a repeated fashion. Have you ever seen a client start to walk through a doorway, stop, start again, and repeat that several times? Or ask you what time lunch is today... then ask you again 5 minutes later... and again 5 minutes after that and they just can't focus on much of anything else? That's perseveration.

Many of our clients don't have those basic skills I just mentioned, so they end up perseverating and/or tantrumming. Can't they learn all those things in a supported living arrangement? Probably... although one reason we have all staff work with all clients is because many clients learn differently than we do, and they might pick up something from you that I didn't do, or they might pick up something from their peer because, "Hey, if he can do it, I can do it," or because they don't take directions well from an authority figure (you, the staff person) but they might from being mentored by a peer. One of the benefits of group training is peer feedback. We have seen a number of times how a behavior can change when a client's peers say, "Hey, Lucy, that's just crazy. Don't do that!" Working with a single staff most of the time may not offer some of those same learning opportunities.

A typical day for our staff (oh, sure, like there's anything resembling a "typical" day) might look like this:

Staff arrives at 8 am and starts making up what they think the day's schedule might look like; "How about I see if Jim, Bob and Mary might like to go out with me today?" Then they look up to see what Objectives Jim, Bob and Mary are working on. Jim has an Objective for riding public transit, Mary has one about street crossing skills, and Bob has one about making a purchase in a store. Go with me, I'm just making this up.

Staff would then say to themselves, "Gee, if we get on the bus and go to K-Mart, we can cover all those skills. Then when the clients arrive, the staff person asks Jim, Bob and Mary, "Hey, you guys, how would you like to go to K-Mart with me today?" They do not announce, "Jim, Bob and Mary, you are with me today. We're going to K-Mart." Where is any personal choice in that?

Any one or all three have the right to say, "Nope. Not today."

"Why not, Jim? You said that you want to go visit your grandmother in Nebraska someday, and that you want to learn how to ride the bus to get there. Well, we can work on your bus skills on the way to K-Mart."

It doesn't matter what Jim gives as a reason why he doesn't want to go. "Those guys are going to the marsh to go bird watching and I want to go with them." That's OK. Staff just goes to that group and says, "Hey, Jim wants to go to the marsh with you guys. Is there anybody that would rather go shopping with us?"

That's why our scheduling is done on a dry erase board. Everyone gets to make a choice to do what they want, as much as possible. Sometimes it doesn't work out. "I'm sorry, Larry, no one is headed to the Go-Go Club today. We're not actually allowed to get drunk during program hours, anyway. Yes, I know that Lisa who used to come here is appearing there topless today...."

But say Jim, Bob and Mary all agree to go to K-Mart. Staff and the group then sits down and does a couple of things while they wait for the transit bus. They make out a list of things to do near K-Mart – other stores that might be fun to go to. This allows clients to actively participate in scheduling the day's activities, and also creates a written itinerary which will lessen transition times while out in the community. The itinerary is not carved in stone, though. Spontaneity can be a good thing.

They could also get out the SNAP Curriculum and review some things like Handling Transfers (for the bus), or Body Language, or Coping with Changes in Routine, or any of over 200 topics. Keep in mind, this is a review and we don't expect clients to "get it" just from a brief interactive discussion. But very often, a review just before putting the skill into practice is very helpful.

Then they get on the bus. The staff person would sit with Jim so they could work on whatever bus skills he has – notifying the driver of your stop, for example. How does the driver know that you want to get off at a particular location? Bob and Mary could sit nearby and hear all this discussion and watch Jim find and pull the cord, too.

Then once off the bus, staff works with Mary about pushing the button to turn the light green. Again, Jim and Bob are standing right there hearing all this information, also. Remember, if you are using a prompting hierarchy, don't repeat prompts. Start with the lowest level prompt, wait a couple of seconds for a response, then move on to the next higher prompt.

When they get to K-Mart, staff works with Bob about how to find socks in the store. Don't know where? Who could we ask… that lady with a shopping cart full of stuff, or the guy in the blue vest? Jim and Mary hang on every word, eager to gain this information, as well.

When they are finished with the basic skills training, they go on with their day, following the itinerary they created earlier, doing whatever other regular folks do in town; more shopping, paying bills, cashing a check, having coffee at the coffee shop, stopping by the art gallery, getting stamps at the post office, stopping by the local senior center to play cards with some lonely elderly folks for a while. That's all we are trying to do – give people with developmental disabilities the opportunity to do regular things where other regular people do them.

In our program, we offer skills training in Community Resources – including public transit, services such as the bank and post office, shopping skills, street safety, and community surroundings (landmarks, where am I? community safety signs, etc.).

Independent Living Skills – including self advocacy issues, emotions (identifying and dealing with), living skills such as renting an apartment, medications, using a phone, making and keeping appointments, nutrition, hygiene, personal care, math/ money skills, adult education, communication skills such as how do I tell people what I want? How do I tell people what I don't want? Interpreting what people say, making choices, criticism (giving and accepting), manners, building trust, personal safety, stranger awareness, social skills/manners, civics, and lots more.

Leisure – including age appropriate art projects (we don't sit and make paper chains all day. Do you ever do that with your adult friends? "Hey, you guys, c'mon over this evening. We'll have a few beers and make paper chains for 3 hours."), relaxation, and visiting local parks and museums and art galleries are all things that we offer that all kinds of people do in our community. Whenever possible (and that would be most of the time), we attend craft classes in town where other people attend craft classes. If a group wants to go bowling, we can do that, but we don't have a time set aside every week where we go bowling at times when the general public isn't around, and if anyone *is* around, they bowl on the other end of the bowling alley to be away from our group. That's not very community inclusive.

Please remember that "mall therapy" (yeah, you know what I'm talking about) really isn't a model of community inclusion. Just hanging out where other people do isn't inclusion unless there is a realistic expectation of interaction with other community members. We're on to that one, buster. That's basic babysitting 101 and we don't do that. We are a training program.

Vocational Skills – punctuality and attendance, dress and hygiene, getting on with other workers, what kind of job do I want? What kinds of jobs are there? Job searching, and basic work ethics.

Again, it's all about all the things that you and I take for granted every day. In our job, though, we have to think about the things we don't think about.

This is no where close to a complete list of skills we regularly work on, but it gives you an idea. The idea is to give our clients as wide of a range of exposure to our communities as possible, and to let the community interact with us and get used to the fact that we are just people living here like everybody else. Are these skills that could be learned in settings other than a day program? Of course. I am not claiming that day programs are the end all. Choices are what we are all about... including choices of services.

Do programs like ours keep people with disabilities segregated as some suggest? No more than public schools segregate children from the rest of society. No more than a factory in an industrial park is segregated. Is a group home located in a neighborhood considered segregation? No more than my house is... it's not open to the public-at large-either.

We work on a huge variety of social skills whether a client has a specific ISP Objective to work on them or not... hygiene, for example. We regularly talk about washing your hands. Every time we sit on a picnic table with bird poop on it, we talk about hygiene. Every time we break for lunch after sorting and shredding confidential documents, we talk about hygiene. Remember to keep your reminders age appropriate… "OK, Susie, you can't eat until you go wash your hands," is how we talk to kids. "Hey, Susie, I'm going to go wash up before lunch, want to come with me?" might be a better way.

We are constantly on the lookout for "teaching moments." That's where something comes up during the day that staff can say, "Wow, did you see that guy throw his trash on the ground? What's that called, when you don't throw your trash in a trash can like that? Oh, yeah, littering…" and they have a whole new topic to review with their clients.

"Jim, you did really good in there when you were talking to that guy. What's that called when you stand a small distance away from someone instead of getting in their face? Oh, yeah, personal space…"

The topic may not have anything at all to do with anyone's ISP Objectives in your group, but there are some subjects that are very helpful to review on a regular basis.

That's the nice thing about the SNAP Curriculum… it's designed to take into the community with you. Each piece is only about 10 minutes long or so. You can talk about these issues anywhere, anytime. We have a man who has a history of stealing. When we go into town to do some shopping, we take a minute to talk to him – and the people with him so we aren't targeting him to make him feel bad or for others to tease him – about stealing. "Hey, you guys, if you take something from a store and don't pay for it, what's that called? Oh, yeah, stealing. What could happen if…?" We don't cover it before going into every store all day long; just once a day if he chooses to go shopping.

His incidents of stealing have dropped to almost zero when he is with us. Remember the discussion about generalization? He still steals at home.

One of my favorites is the man in our program who has

an ISP Objective to mentor his peers about safe street crossing skills. Mark has great street crossing skills, so we let him show his peers how he does it. This teaches Mark the difference between mentoring and "bossing." And it lets his peers learn from someone other than an authority figure. Where do we work on these skills? Not in our facility. There aren't any crosswalks in our building.

Communication skills are what we work on the most. Non-verbal people can't tell you and often don't know how to tell you things in another appropriate way, and verbal people often just don't have the skill to say what they actually mean. Remember the guy who was labeled "mad" when he was really uncomfortable? He was verbal and you could carry on a fine conversation with him.

Recently our adult education teacher created a picture book with the assistance of several clients. The book is full of photographs of local stores in the surrounding towns. The book was created specifically for a deaf, non-verbal man named Ron to be able to communicate his daily choice of where he would like to go, but we were surprised at how quickly other clients latched on to the book. Verbal, non-verbal, it doesn't matter. Almost everybody likes to use these books. I think we are up to 3 books of stores, parks, museums... all the places that people go to every day.

We are in the process of creating an icon board so people can tell us a variety of things – pain levels, emotions, etc. The board is specifically for Ron, but we are going to mount the board (or a couple of them throughout the building) and let him know that the boards are for everyone, not "just for him because he has trouble communicating." There is no reason to target Ron outwardly and point out his differences to him. I suspect he is already aware of his differences. We don't need to highlight them for him.

We believe that a photograph often works better as an icon than a drawing. Which says, "I want to go to Safeway" better

- a drawing of a cartoon person standing in front of a stand of vegetables, or a photograph of the client standing in front of Safeway (or whatever grocery store you have where you live)? "Oh, that's me and that's where I want to be."

I mentioned the prompting hierarchy a couple of times. That's the instructional process we generally use. It's just a sequence of verbal/auditory, visual, and/or hands on cues given to get an individual to begin or complete a task.

Our goal is for the person to do a task following a natural cue. The light turns green and we go. The alarm goes off and we get up. The buzzer goes off and we take the cupcakes out of the oven.

My wife taking cookies out of the oven seems to be a natural cue for me to immediately pop one in my mouth... then dance around whimpering, " Haaaht! Ith haaaht!"

With clients, we often have to use a series of prompts to get them used to doing the task or behavior. Our hope is that they eventually fade to a natural cue/prompt.

We use the following series – you might use something like this or something with completely different names. It doesn't matter what you call your prompts. Just make sure your staff are all using the same thing:

Gestural – You (the staff person) point to the clock so that the client looks up and sees that it is noon. They go get their lunch to eat.

Indirect Verbal – You say, "Hey, what time is it?" as a cue for the client to make the connection between it being 12:00 and being time to go get their lunch and eat.

Direct Verbal – You say, "It's 12:00. That's lunchtime. Let's eat."

Model – You get out your lunch and start to eat while the client observes and mimics your actions.

Minimal Physical – You put the client's sandwich on a plate for them.

Partial Physical – You put their sandwich in their hand.

Full Physical – You cut up the client's sandwich and feed it to them.

Notice that each prompt is a little more restrictive than the one previous. Always start with the least restrictive prompt in an individual's hierarchy. If their individual hierarchy is something like "gestural-indirect verbal-direct verbal", start with the gestural to see if they can do it. Start with this prompt every time. Never begin with the prompt that you are most certain that they will respond to. Give them the opportunity to do the task with the least restrictive prompt. If they don't respond to the gestural prompt after a couple of seconds, go to the next higher level (more restrictive) prompt; in this case, an indirect verbal. Again, wait a couple of seconds to give them a chance to respond, then move on to the next level if necessary.

If the client fails to do the task after the final prompt, record a "Failed Trial" and try again later.

Make sure you can distinguish a Failed Trial from a Refusal. A Failed Trial means that they made some attempt, but couldn't finish or finished incorrectly. A Refusal means that they didn't even give it the old college try. They ignored you, turned away, hit you... whatever their sign of refusing is. Don't judge them if they refuse or fail. Just try it again later. You might have to make some adjustments in the time, location, or other environmental conditions surrounding the trial.

The trick is, the series of prompts must be individualized. No client is going to require the entire list of prompts we use.

Work with the client to see what their current baseline is. Ah! There *was* a point to baselines.

The biggest mistake I see staff make is giving prompts in combination. Don't use a gestural prompt, pointing to the clock, and say, "What time is it?" You just gave them 2 prompts. How will you know which one they are responding to? I have seen staff slap their own hand for doing that.

And again, do not repeat prompts. We aren't trying to teach Justine to cross the street after every third prompt. Give a prompt once, and then move on… unless you are sure Justine didn't hear you. Then you can repeat.

Some staff thinks this process in more complicated than it really is. If the individual's hierarchy is only 3 prompts, then it takes 6 – 10 seconds to practice the skill with the prompting hierarchy. After giving the instructional cue:

1. Staff points to the button to change the crosswalk sign (a gestural prompt). Staff waits approximately 2 seconds. No response.

2. "Bob, how do we get the sign to change?" (an indirect verbal prompt). Wait approximately 2 seconds. No response.

3. "Bob, push the button so the light will change." (a direct verbal prompt).

If Bob pushes the button at any point in the hierarchy, deliver the reinforcer, write down which prompt was the successful one, and stop giving prompts. If Bob doesn't respond correctly with any prompts, record a failed trial. If Bob makes it clear that he isn't going to work on this skill right now, (he turns and walks away from the corner, etc), then record a refusal.

That's all there is to it. Not really complicated at all. We call this process a "trial". A plan may specify that a client should be offered a "trial" once per day, or twice per week, or whatever.

Give some thought to where you can realistically use a

prompting hierarchy. Are you going to use it to teach money counting skills in line at the grocery store? Probably not. You don't want to hold up the line for other customers and you don't want to be waving a big red flag attracting attention to the fact that you are "working with this person with a disability".

We might use a prompting hierarchy when shaping a behavior. Shaping involves reinforcing successive approximations of a desired behavior – that is, rewarding those forms of behavior that most closely approximate the target response until the appropriate behavior is learned. Shaping is not in itself a method for teaching replacement behaviors. It is a method that assists you in setting goals for the behavior. You define steps that lead to the appropriate behavior.

We worked with a man who liked to go behind counters in stores. If there was an item for sale on the shelf, this guy was convinced that there had to be a better one hidden behind the counter...and he would push his way to get there. Store clerks generally didn't like this.

We set up a series of steps that would lead to him not going behind counters.

1. Communicate his intentions with an observable sign (verbal or not).
2. Recognize limited entry signs such as "keep out" or "no trespassing", etc.
3. Immediately leave an unauthorized area when prompted.
4. Not enter unauthorized areas.

I heard a good explanation of shaping - when playing the game "Hot and Cold", you reward any movement that takes the player closer to the prize by saying "hotter." Each successive movement is a closer approximation of the desired behavior. If the prize is in the closet, and the player is moving toward the closet, every time the player takes a step toward the closet, you yell "hotter!", and you are reinforcing the behavior. If the player moves away from the closet, you yell, "colder!" (non-reinforcing).

If the client communicates his intention (the example above), you yell "hotter!" (or maybe "good job, Bob!") (positive reinforcement) and once he is doing that consistently, you stop reinforcing that step and you yell "hotter" when he looks at or points to signs that state unauthorized areas (even if he doesn't obey them yet) until he is doing that consistently… etc., until he doesn't go in unauthorized areas. And, of course, you wouldn't yell the reinforcer at him. If he falls back and doesn't communicate his intentions anymore, go back and start again. But this is a way Bob could learn not to go where he isn't supposed to.

You might start with the behavior step that is already closest to being in the individual's repertoire. This is really simplified, but I hope you get the idea.

Chaining is another process - forward, backward or global chaining. In forward chaining, the client does the first step of a process (such as washing their hands), and staff assists or does the remaining steps, in order. This is repeated until the client is great at the first step. Then the client does the first two steps and staff does/assists with the remaining steps until the client can do the first two well, then the client does the first three steps, etc.

Again, you might use a prompting hierarchy to actually teach the individual steps.

Backward chaining is the same basic process, but starting with the last step in a process and moving forward. This may be used when a client needs the immediate reward of the finished process to even work on a chain (such as receiving the soda from a soda machine before learning to push the correct button and put the correct amount of change in the machine, etc.). Staff does the first steps and the client does the last step. Then staff does all but the last 2 steps, etc.

Global chaining is where you start with the step that the client can already do no matter where in the chain it is and it doesn't matter what order you teach the steps. Just make sure the client understands that the steps do need to eventually go in order.

There are other methods such as a Discrete Trial. This is a pairing of prompts with success or failed trial without further prompting. Discrete Trials pretty much have to be done on a 1:1 basis and you would receive special training before using one.

Understanding which instructional process to use is an important step for staff and clients. If you don't truly understand the concepts, that's OK. Start right now. Don't worry about what you did wrong yesterday. Look up information on the prompting hierarchy, chaining, and shaping and other processes. Start with the internet.

We also use an "Instructional Cue" to let the client know that we are about to give the task a try. Don't surprise a client and wonder why they don't respond. This is just some phrase that alerts them that you have some expectation of them working on the specific skill now… "Bob, let's work on your street crossing skill when we get to the corner."

Chapter 11 – Vocational Training

Vocational Training. This is an extremely popular issue right now. Can people learn vocational skills in a day program or a sheltered workshop? Yes. Yes they can. We currently offer our clients the opportunity to learn some basic job skills while earning a wage. The wage is often less than minimum wage. GASP!

We pay our employees (staff) minimum wage… or a little above… we're at the mercy of the State for funding. We have certain qualifications that we require they meet before we will hire them and pay them that wage. We pay the trainees (clients) in our program a commensurate wage. A commensurate wage is determined by surveying other businesses in the area that pay employees to do a similar job – say confidential document disposal, since that's what we offer.

What? Shredding paper? That's not a real job!

Really? Most of our customers think it is when they worry about identity theft. That's why they come to us. We're about the only game in town for shredding documents on any scale. We charge competitive rates with the other couple of places that do it. No one thinks of using our services because we "don't pay our clients anything so we can shred paper cheap." They use our service because we are competitively priced, we show up when we say we're going to, and we finish jobs in a timely manner. But about wages…

The wages we surveyed in the area are averaged and we come up with a "prevailing wage." At the same time, we go through a process of breaking down our confidential document disposal job into a series of job elements/tasks. For example; picking up the paper from a business may include choosing the appropriate boxes, carrying them a certain distance, weighing and documenting the weight, etc. We then have a couple of people who are really good at this (staff or clients) go through the process. This sets a standard for a rating that the client also performs. The client's time and errors are judged against the standard to see how much of the job they can perform and how well. They are then paid a wage based on what they can do, while they learn the skills needed to do the complete job. The rating process is repeated every six months or when we see a change in the client that tells us they may be doing worse or better for any reason... or when the client asks to have another rating. This is certainly a simplified description of the process, but it's the basics.

When I started every job I have ever held, the employer assumed I already had the most basic of job skills and I suspect they wouldn't have kept me on the payroll very long in order to pay me a full wage while I learned to accept instructions from a supervisor, or not to spit on my co-worker because they are staring at me. When I hire a staff person, I assume they already have basic job skills. That's why we require minimum qualifications to hire. The wages we pay clients/trainees are not intended to be living wages. They are an incentive to keep learning new functional skills.

Clients who choose to work in our program don't have the usual required minimum qualifications.

We have several clients who make the current minimum wage. They have learned most of the basic skills and are getting pretty good at the job. Does that mean they are ready to leave us, get their own apartment and get a job at General Electric? Not necessarily. It means that they have learned most of the basics required towards meeting minimum requirements for a job of some sort.

Do I view this process as "using clients as slave labor"? Please. If you actually believe that, then you truly don't have an understanding of the process. I view it as giving clients an opportunity to earn a monetary incentive while learning a new skill which may help them reach their desired stated long range goal of having a job someday.

You *do* know that not everybody makes the same wage in "real life", right? People are paid on their experience, their productivity, their seniority…

We start the process in the client's ISP meeting. "Stuart, what do you want for someday in your life?"

"I want a job at McDonald's because I really like eating hamburgers."

"What do you want to do at McDonald's?"

"Eat hamburgers, I just told you that."

"I don't think they pay people to do that, Stuart. Are you interested in making hamburgers or selling them to customers, or…?"

"Yeah, making them."

"What does that mean to you… making hamburgers?"

"Cooking them and putting them together."

"Do you know how to do that?"

"I know the paper wrapper goes on the outside."

"What do you think it takes to have a job like that?"

"I don't know."

"Would you like to learn some basic job skills that might help you get a job there someday?"

"Yeah."

"Would you like to earn some money while you learn about having a job?"

"Yeah!"

"The job we offer doesn't have anything directly to do with making hamburgers. You would learn some skills like showing up to a workroom on time, notifying us if you can't make it to work, and how to stick with a task until it is finished and things like that. Is that OK?"

"Stick with a task?"

"Yeah, if you are making hamburgers, you can't put most of the stuff on it and then stop because you would rather make french fries. You would have to stick with the task of making the hamburger until it is finished."

"OK."

"You may make less money than other people make for doing the same thing. Your wage will be based on what you *can* do while you learn more. Do you understand that? Do you have any questions about it?"

"OK."

I know that some people have a problem with teaching a client to stick to task, but as an employer, I really prefer people who finish what they start… and finish it in a timely manner. It doesn't work for me if I hear a staff person say, "Ally, I know your hands are all wet and soapy, but you can finish learning to wash your hands later. I want to do an art project right now. Your hands will dry out eventually."

Do many sheltered workshops around the country have a problem with "down time"… periods of time when there is no work available? Yep. Do many workshops let people sit around and do nothing during these times? Yep. Do those staff people have enough training of their own? Apparently not. Whose fault is that? Don't care. But it's time for them to step up and do something about it.

We're lucky in that our main purpose is to teach social and behavioral skills, so when we have no paid work available we just close our workroom and go on with other activities.

Maybe workshops could think about this problem before it comes up (an advanced technical process called "planning ahead") and have materials available to, say, assist clients to gather personal information that they will use on a resume, or talk about what a job interview might be like… what kinds of questions an employer might ask and what some possible answers to those questions might be (this is covered in the SNAP Curriculum), or video tape a mock interview so the client can see how they appear to a potential employer… there are lots of vocational issues.

I absolutely agree that having a client sit and "practice sorting the same bunch of paper clips over and over" is ridiculous. I guess it kills time, but you might want to keep the term "functional" in mind. If you don't teach that client to sort those same paperclips over and over, will someone have to do it for them? Are you trying to bore them to death? Do you really want them to think that's what "having a job" means?

For the people thinking, "I told you that sheltered workshops don't work," why are the funders of these programs unable to understand either market fluctuations or the concept of small towns without a lot of work? Why aren't vocational programs allowed to do other activities when there is "down time"? I had a wood working business of my own for a couple of years. I also had some "down times". I made garden related products and people where I live don't garden all year long. It's even worse where I grew up in the Sierra Nevadas where it snows in the winter. Then no one gardens. When I had no orders, I did other things… I read a book, I practiced magic tricks and my banjo…just like sheltered workshops should be allowed to do without pressure to "stay busy"! But that's just my personal opinion. You *do* have a banjo at your program, don't you?

By the way, do you have your clients fill out an application and go through an interview in order to start work in your program? Why not? Do your clients fill out their own time cards or does staff do that for them? Just a thought.

Do you offer clients the opportunity to participate in volunteer jobs in the community? We do from time to time… but we took those out of our "vocational" folder and put them in our "civics" folder. For us, volunteering at the local humane society or wherever has as much to do with teaching a person to be a responsible neighbor in our community as it does teaching job skills. Although we take our volunteer jobs very seriously and it's a good opportunity to teach clients about personal responsibility (work ethics) as well as other "vocational" skills.

Are "vocational" and "civics" just labels? Yep. It really doesn't matter what we call the skills. If the client is interested in learning them, we teach them. The labels are just for our convenience.

Chapter 12 – Data Collection

No discussion of all these issues would be complete without mentioning data collection. No job is complete until the paperwork is finished. Very often, no job is even started until the paperwork is finished. Sometimes we bury ourselves in paperwork... and sometimes paperwork is absolutely necessary. Thank goodness for computers so we have a paperless society... or so they say.

Data collection refers to all the methods we use to assess and keep track of behaviors and skills. Data collection allows us to measure behavior and determine the effectiveness of treatment plans as well as being able to determine when a plan really started working or when it stopped working. Data collection allows us to formulate a hypothesis (a good guess) about behavior functions, gives us a way to analyze results of treatment plans, and it helps keep all team members informed about behavioral changes.

"In the beginning..." there were assessments. You can't write a treatment plan – ISP, Behavior Support Plan, or any other kind of plan – and therefore you can't track progress – until you have established some sort of a baseline for the client's behaviors and skills. You would be surprised at how useless a "good guess" is regarding baseline information. "Tricia has pretty good street crossing skills," doesn't tell us anything about Tricia's street crossing skills. "Bob hits others," doesn't tell us anything about the frequency, duration or intensity of the behavior. "Marcy wants to learn to read," is interesting, but it doesn't tell us if she can currently read at the first grade level or the sixth grade level.

Once we have a baseline and we have written a terrific treatment plan, we have to have a method of tracking progress or the lack thereof on each person's goals and objectives.

I have mentioned baselines a couple of times. Let me elaborate...

Susan's support team all agree that she could benefit from using a way of communicating other than using assaultive behaviors. Currently, when she wants to go shopping instead of participating in a nutrition activity, she will spit at people around her. We cannot write a plan to change the spitting behavior until we have some clue as to why she spits instead of asking to change groups. It's easy to say, "Well, obviously, she doesn't want to participate in the nutrition activity."

Are you sure? Is it the nutrition activity per se or is it the time and location of the nutrition activity? Does she spit at all staff who offer her the opportunity to participate, or just male staff? Or just at you? Will she participate in the activity on Tuesdays but not Wednesdays? How does she make her choice of other activities known? Is spitting her way of saying, "No thank you, I would rather do *this* right now,"?

The answers to this and other questions will tell us her baseline behavior. You may discover that she spits at transition times for any activity. Very often, data collection will let you know that behaviors that are reported by staff as happening "all the time" actually don't happen all the time. "Jim hit other people all day." Really? From the time he stepped off of his transportation this morning until he went home, he never stopped hitting? And you let this go on?

Baseline data must be gathered under as natural conditions as possible. If Jim hits "all day" when he rides the public transit bus, then it won't be helpful to observe Jim in your facility.

Data must be collected for a long enough of a period to be useful, too. Collecting data during a period when the behavior doesn't typically occur is pretty much useless. "Nope, I didn't see it happen."

There are tons of assessments and types of recording methods. We looked at lots of forms and then changed them around to meet our needs. We have a Learning Skills Assessment to help us identify the manner in which a person is best able to learn skills, Are they a visual learner (can watch someone do it and repeat it), or an auditory learner (can hear instructions and can do it), or a kinetic learner (hands on)? Most of us use a combination of those methods.

We use a Training Preference Assessment to identify how an individual responds best while participating in training activities. Do they prefer male or female staff? Do they respond well to mixed gender peer groups? Are they generally more alert in the morning or afternoon? Clients, like most of us, learn best when we are where we want to be with people we want to be with.

We require staff to fill out annual Community Safety Assessments regarding client street safety and stranger awareness skills.

We also require staff to complete a Reinforcer Assessment for/with their clients. This identifies specific individualized reinforcers to which a client responds positively for day to day training activities. What specific phrase, if any, works well for Robert, who prefers verbal praise as his social reinforcer?

We make extensive use of ABC Assessments for behavioral issues:

Antecedent: What was going on prior to the behavior? Who was around? Was it noisy? How long had the client been walking before they suddenly tripped you, out of the blue?

Behavior: What did you see that caused you to mention the behavior as a problem? What is the Topography of the behavior? (You can do this… chapter 2).

Consequence: What happened following the behavior? What did you do? What did the client do? What did you say? How did the client react?

Motivational Assessments are used to determine why a client may be engaging in a specific behavior. It identifies situations in which a person is likely to behave in certain ways, such as escaping demands, looking for sensory input, seeking tangible things, etc.

Scatter Plot Assessments are used to find patterns in a specific behavior; specifically times in which a behavior occurs. If Rich displays assaultive behaviors often at 11:00 and he takes his medications at 12:00, there's a clue.

We also make extensive use of a Future Life Plan. This document is filled out by the client with staff assistance, and it talks about the individual's upcoming ISP meeting. It gives staff a chance to review some self advocacy issues with the client and it encourages the client to write down how they think they have done on their Objectives this past year (or whatever time table they are on) as well as writing down any new ideas of what they would like to work on next. We have observed very often that when a client gets into their ISP meeting with a bunch of people around – hopefully people that they have invited – they are suddenly like a deer in the headlights. They clam up. I love mixing metaphors. With their Future Life Plan in hand, they can be reminded that "didn't you tell me that you wanted to learn to...?"

Yes, you in the back with your hand up? What? You don't have all those fancy forms? If you don't have any of these assessments, do not despair. Get on the internet and look at what other people use, then adapt them to suit your needs. It's unfortunate that there isn't more discussion/action about training, and I feel like I spend most of my time reinventing the wheel, but that's where we are. And what I can do about it is to try to let other people know that they aren't alone and that there are ways to make your program an effective one, no matter what you might hear and read. Start making changes. Small ones. There is no need to shut down your program and start fresh. Fix this and fix that, and pretty soon, you'll have an effective, client driven program.

More data recording forms for you to worry that you don't have:

Frequency Count – mark every time a behavior occurs in a predetermined period of time. This gives you answers such as, "Jessica rocks her body 6 times per hour," or "Bill shreds 22 pounds of paper in an hour."

Duration Recording – measures how long a behavior lasts, or another way, the amount of time a person spends doing something whether it is a tantrum or practicing writing skills. "Rebecca's tantrum lasted 2 minutes." You must define the cycle of a behavior for this to work. For example, a "tantrum" ends when Rebecca ceases yelling and/or stops rolling on the floor for one or more minutes. Then you can record how long a single tantrum lasted.

Latency Recording – how much time lapsed between the time you gave an instructional cue and when the client began the task/behavior or when they finished the task/behavior? This is helpful when working on behaviors such as lengthening the time Ryan stays calm when presented with a request to accept delay in the fulfillment of a personal request. "I want to use the computer, and I want to use it now!"

Interval Recording – helpful for recording continuous behaviors such as a client who keeps their hand in their mouth for long periods of time. An observation period is divided up into an equal number of intervals. In Whole Interval Recording, you would track a behavior if it occurred continuously throughout the observational period (such as hand flapping). For Partial Interval Recording, you would track the behavior if it occurs at all during the observation period.

Time Sampling - records the presence or absence of a behavior by recording whether or not the behavior is present at the end of a predetermined time period.

Don't worry if you don't know what I'm talking about. Get on the internet and look this stuff up.

We also make extensive use of case notes. These are notes written by staff regarding unusual behaviors they have observed throughout the day. It's anecdotal data. It's a way to keep all staff members informed about client issues as they happen. Our case note forms are set up in an A-B-C (antecedent-behavior-consequence) format. Some places just let staff write a "story" about what happened. Use whatever works for you and your staff. All of our staff have to read and initial every case note every two weeks. All staff work with all clients in our program and it makes a difference for them to know what is currently going on with each client. It's just a good way to keep everyone informed, as well as a way for us to track behavior issues another way. It isn't unusual for our Resource Specialist to look back through case notes and see that a pattern is developing in a new behavior and maybe it's time to start a plan or at least a specific behavioral tracking sheet.

And we use what we call "tracking sheets." Some people call it charting. They are just forms where staff can record what happened with each person's ISP Objectives for the day. Did the person have an opportunity to work on their skills today? Did they accept or refuse? What was the highest level of prompting (not how many prompts!) they required for this task today? And whatever other information will be necessary to determine if the plan is working or not. Did a particular behavior occur today? How many times? What intensity? Is the individual making progress or do we have to evaluate their current skill and motivation level. Do we have to look at staff's skill and motivation level?

We use the information from the tracking sheets to write reviews so all of the client's support team members can see what is going on. Staff have a daily record to review and see if the level of prompting never seems to change. A flat line across means that something isn't working. The client's support team members get a copy of the review to peruse at least every six months.

One of the biggest problems we have with staff is that they are always hesitant to question things. It is OK for a staff person to question an ISP when they get a new one. "Hey, this says that we are going to teach Steve to keep drool wiped off his face, but he has no feeling on that side of his face and he can't tell when he is drooling." The plan probably made perfect sense to us in the office when we wrote it, but it may not make as much sense to the line staff implementing the plan.

My suspicion is that staff people don't want to appear as though they don't know what they are doing. Heck, none of us know what we are doing for sure. If someone claims to be an expert and they know exactly what a client needs, count the fingers on your hand when they leave to make sure you still have them all. And I think legally, you have 3 days to return that bottle of snake oil.

All of this is all more than just a way to keep a job for someone. I know there are some in our own field who make those kinds of accusations – that we "keep clients in our programs in order to keep our own jobs." That is so sad and so cynical.

Chapter 13 – To Sum Up

Are there programs that don't work well? Of course, but that isn't necessarily a reason to make blanket statements about segregation and mistreatment of people and jump on a bandwagon of change. Let's not throw out the baby with the bath water.

I had thought that we were past the point of making sure all people with developmental disabilities are in the same box, but apparently I was wrong (darn, first time, too).

Don't get me wrong... some bandwagons are good. My mother's side of our family were circus people (yeah, really). My uncle played on the bandwagon... literally... he was in the band and they played on a bandwagon sometimes. It was a cool bandwagon and everybody loved it. Lots of people jumped on it.

I am not against change. Change brought about the end to the miserable state mental institutions. There are programs still around that treat their clients like children and keep them at their facility all day so that they don't have to deal with public behaviors. Those programs need to change. All I am saying is, everybody take a breath. Are we providing the training needed to produce results that guarantee a range of services available to people with developmental disabilities to meet *their* needs and not what makes *us* feel good or costs the least money?

If there are people out there who had bad experiences

working in bad programs, I'm sorry. Ours is a good program and I heartily invite you to come visit. Your experience may not be indicative of an entirely broken system.

The more those of us actually providing the services can talk to each other and not depend on experts to notify us of the latest "fad in the field," the more this field will change for the better. It takes a commitment from people with their feet on the ground to create the environment for change. Conditions for change are no different for us than they are for people with developmental disabilities. People tend to change when:

- They have participated in the decision to change,
- They see other people changing,
- They have the competencies, knowledge, or skills required by the change,
- They trust the motives of the person suggesting the changes,
- They see the change has been successful.

People who write books complaining, but not offering any suggestions for solutions, still serve a purpose if what they write gets people thinking and questioning. Those who offer solutions are a step ahead and are more likely to be listened to and have an impact on the care and education of people with developmental disabilities.

I stated in the beginning that I am not an expert in this field. I am just a guy trying to do a good job and wanting to share what I have learned with others. I am certainly not looking for anyone to jump on my bandwagon. Every service provider across the country has their own challenges and they have to discover what works best for them and especially what works best for the people they are serving. All I ask is that you take a step back and ask yourself, "Are we doing the best that we can?" If the answer is "no," or worse, "I don't care, it's just a paycheck," then it's time to step up or step out. My fervent hope is that you will step up and think about what you are doing today. "Is there even a small change I can make today to make our service better?"

You may have noticed that most of the behavioral principles mentioned in this book do not just apply to people with developmental disabilities. The principles apply to your coworkers, your spouse and your friends. We all have behaviors and we all use those behaviors to communicate. I hired a woman recently whose husband was recovering from a stroke and had very limited verbal communication skills left. She said that one of the biggest lessons she learned immediately was not to tell her husband, "You need to stop yelling," when he became frustrated at his inability to communicate, but to say, "I need you to stop yelling and help me find a way to understand what you want." Both of their frustration levels dropped considerably with that one small change.

Success stories are small (I didn't say few, I said small) in our field. We aren't going to cure anybody of their developmental disability. I remember the day at one of our client association meetings when a woman got up to make an announcement that she had taken the public transit bus from one town to a neighboring town and back all by herself for the first time. Everyone, peers and staff alike, were cheering.

I remember a staff telling me about how we had been working with Carl for quite a while about handling his own transit ticket. Carl has autism, but he likes going to town. His support team decided to see if Carl couldn't learn a few of the transit skills we all use so that he wouldn't have to be so dependent on someone else to do every thing for him.

We started with a plan to have Carl hold his own ticket. He would take the ticket, look at it and throw it on the ground. Staff would pick it up, hand it back to him and explain why it is important for his to accept responsibility for his own ticket.

He would throw the ticket on the ground and staff would pick it up and hand it back…

Until the day staff handed him his ticket, bent over to pick up the ticket as usual… and there was no ticket. Carl was standing there, holding his ticket with a look on his face like, "What? I've got my ticket." He now holds his ticket until he boards the bus at which time he puts the ticket in the hopper.

One of our biggest success stories is Daniel. Daniel is a man in his 50's. I have worked with him for 10 years. When we were still in our old building with 100 clients, Daniel spent his days in a room with other clients at his same approximate developmental level, spinning in circles, making grunting noises and slapping himself in the face.

When we moved to our smaller facilities, we no longer worried about keeping people with similar developmental levels together (finally!). Daniel goes out with all sorts of people. Instead of spinning in circles, grunting and slapping himself, he keeps an envelope in his locker with money in it. Do I think he knows that it is "money"? I'm not sure. It doesn't matter for now. We know that when he gets the envelope out of his locker and waves it at a staff person, he is saying, "Today, I want to go out to the bakery." He doesn't do that every day, just the days he wants to go to the bakery.

We take him to the bakery and he will point at a cookie or a donut. He knows the difference. And the clerk knows what he is ordering. Daniel knows the money has to go to someone before he gets his cookie or donut – he's still a little unsure about who gets the money – but he finally hands the money over to the clerk to get his item.

This is a huge success for us and an even bigger success for Daniel. And he learned to do these things in a group activity day program.

Do you have a "Daniel" in your program? Are you looking at ways to enable him to order his own darn cookies?

Most of the principles I have talked about in this book

have been simplified. The point is for you to hopefully see something that may be new to you and for you to ask questions and look up more information. Don't take everything I say as gospel, either. I want you to be assertive and find your own successful program.

Oh, and lest I forget, good luck!

The Specific Natural Activity Program (SNAP) Curriculum

SNAP is designed to assist agency staff, counselors, teachers and parents in presenting age appropriate basic skills training for adults with developmental disabilities. This curriculum applies to everyday tasks and deals with more than 200 topics. The material assists in facilitation of discussion of a wide variety of topics in the Daily Living Skills, Community Resource, Vocational and Leisure domains.

Available from Program Development Associates: www. disabilitytraining.com

Individual Service Plan Guidelines

A basic "how to" for writing Individual Service Plans. Step by step explanations for thinking out each component of a plan including Long Range Goals, Objectives, and Criteria. Includes sample assessment forms and questionnaires as well as an introduction to the basics of Instructional Processes.

Available from the author at: ispguide@yahoo.com